NEW DIRECTIONS FOR CHILD AND ADOLESCENT DEVELOPMENT

William Damon, *Stanford University*
EDITOR-IN-CHIEF

Social Exchange
in Development

Brett Laursen
Florida Atlantic University

William G. Graziano
Texas A&M University

EDITORS

Number 95, Spring 2002

JOSSEY-BASS
San Francisco

Social Exchange in Development
Brett Laursen, William G. Graziano (eds.)
New Directions for Child and Adolescent Development, no. 95
William Damon, Editor-in-Chief

Microfilm copies of issues and articles are available in 16mm and 35mm, as well as microfiche in 105mm, through University Microfilms Inc., 300 North Zeeb Road, Ann Arbor, Michigan 48106-1346.

ISSN 1520-3247   electronic ISSN 1534-8687   ISBN 0-7879-6288-0

NEW DIRECTIONS FOR CHILD AND ADOLESCENT DEVELOPMENT is part of The Jossey-Bass Education Series and is published quarterly by Wiley Subscription Services, Inc., a Wiley company, at Jossey-Bass, 989 Market Street, San Francisco, California 94103-1741. Periodicals postage paid at San Francisco, California, and at additional mailing offices. Postmaster: Send address changes to New Directions for Child and Adolescent Development, Jossey-Bass, 989 Market Street, San Francisco, CA 94103-1741.

New Directions for Child and Adolescent Development is indexed in Biosciences Information Service, Current Index to Journals in Education (ERIC), Psychological Abstracts, and Sociological Abstracts.

SUBSCRIPTIONS cost $75.00 for individuals and $144.00 for institutions, agencies, and libraries.

EDITORIAL CORRESPONDENCE should be sent to the Editor-in-Chief, William Damon, Stanford Center on Adolescence, Cypress Building C, Stanford University, Stanford, CA 94305

Cover photograph by Wernher Krutein/PHOTOVAULT © 1990.

Jossey-Bass Web address: www.josseybass.com

Printed in the United States of America on acid-free recycled paper containing 100 percent recovered waste paper, of which at least 20 percent is postconsumer waste.

CONTENTS

Editors' Notes

Ideas come and go. Some have a brief time in the sun and then (to mix metaphors) are consigned to the dustbin of history. There are usually good reasons for discarding an idea. Some ideas depend on assumptions that eventually prove untenable. Some are supplanted by new ones that are more parsimonious. Still others prove to be false. We do not mourn the passing of such ideas because this is the normal course of intellectual progress.

More interesting are ideas that are assumed to be moribund because they fall out of fashion. This volume is concerned with social exchange theory, a family of ideas that has been pronounced dead several times—pronouncements that have all proven premature. Social exchange theory takes a unique perspective on the organization of social interactions and the motives of participants in these interchanges. In so doing, it provides insights on social relations that are absent from other approaches. These insights may be ignored for a time but never disappear altogether.

The chapter authors do not agree on the details concerning social exchange, but then neither did the original proponents of the theory (Homans, 1974; Thibaut and Kelley, 1959; Walster, Walster, and Berscheid, 1978). Nevertheless, they share a few core tenets. The social exchange process is basic to all human social relations. Because no individual is entirely self-sufficient, he or she must exchange resources with others in order to survive and reproduce. These interpersonal exchanges, evident in all cultures, facilitate coordinated social behavior (Harris, 1968). When social exchanges become routine, norms may evolve around them. This volume is primarily concerned with the origins of social exchange processes and the norms associated them.

In the not-too-distant past, the enculturation of children was seen as a simple process: children learned behaviors as they experienced culture. The first generation of theorists in this learning approach to social development assumed that external reinforcement was critical and was probably tied to the reduction of some internal drive state (Sears, Maccoby, and Levin, 1957). This view passed away under the weight of facts to the contrary. Later views reframed learning as a more cognitive process, allowing for observational learning, internal mental states, and expectations (Bandura, 1971; Hartup and Yonas, 1971). Eventually, this social learning view was supplanted (not replaced) by a view that incorporated the child's relationship context (Cairns, 1979). Seen in this light, perhaps it is not surprising that the chapter authors all share the assumption that relationships provide the critical context for social exchange process.

This volume demonstrates that social exchange theory continues to offer a viable, even unique, perspective on human social relations. We hope that it will stimulate renewed interest in social exchange processes among those who are interested in understanding relationships and their development.

William G. Graziano
Brett Laursen
Editors

References

Bandura, A. (ed.). *Psychological Modeling: Conflicting Theories.* New York: Aldine de Gruyter, 1971.

Cairns, R. B. *Social Development: The Origins and Plasticity of Interchanges.* New York: Freeman, 1979.

Harris, M. *The Rise of Anthropological Theory: A History of Theories of Culture.* New York: Crowell, 1968.

Hartup, W. W., and Yonas, A. "Developmental Psychology." *Annual Review of Psychology,* 1971, *22,* 337–392.

Homans, G. *Social Behavior: Its Elementary Forms.* (Rev. ed.) New York: Harcourt, 1974.

Sears, R. R., Maccoby, E. S., and Levin, H. *Patterns of Child Rearing.* New York: Harper-Collins, 1957.

Thibaut, J. W., and Kelley, H. H. *The Social Psychology of Groups.* New York: Wiley, 1959.

Walster, E., Walster, G. W., and Berscheid, E. S. *Equity: Theory and Research.* Needham Heights, Mass.: Allyn & Bacon, 1978.

WILLIAM G. GRAZIANO *is professor of psychology at Texas A&M University.*

BRETT LAURSEN *is professor of psychology at Florida Atlantic University.*

1

This chapter describes the use of communal norms that dictate noncontingent responsiveness to a partner's needs and advances propositions about the mechanisms that promote their development.

Adherence to Communal Norms: What It Means, When It Occurs, and Some Thoughts on How It Develops

Margaret S. Clark, Sarah D. Jordan

This chapter deals with communal norms governing the giving and acceptance of benefits in relationships. We define benefits as something of value one person intentionally gives to another person, such as gifts, services, compliments, instructions, and emotional support. This definition excludes rewards derived from relationships that one person does not intentionally give to the other, such as the pride a person might feel at being seen in public with an attractive partner.

Communal norms dictate noncontingent, need-based giving and accepting of benefits. They apply to select relationships up to implicit cost levels that vary by relationship. From the perspective of potential donors of benefits, communal norms dictate concern for the welfare of one's partner and benefiting that partner in response to his or her needs without requiring repayments. From the perspective of potential recipients of benefits, communal norms call for being open about needs, seeking benefits when they are needed, and accepting needed help without believing one must repay that help.

Preparation of this chapter and some of the empirical work cited was supported by a grant from the National Science Foundation (9983417) and an REU supplement to that grant. Any opinions, findings, conclusions, or recommendations expressed are those of the authors and do not necessarily reflect the views of the National Science Foundation.

The Difference Between Communal and Exchange Relationships

Qualitative and quantitative distinctions between communal and exchange relationships have been advanced. Following is a brief overview of the history of these constructs.

The Original, Qualitative Distinction. In an early article, Clark and Mills (1979) argued that in communal relationships, people feel a desire or obligation to be responsive to one another's needs. In these relationships, people give benefits in response to needs without expecting repayment. In many other relationships, people prefer to operate on what Clark and Mills (1979) called an exchange basis: they give benefits expecting to receive comparable benefits in return.

In the original experimental studies supporting the distinction, students at a university were assigned randomly to a communal or an exchange condition. Those assigned to the communal condition were led to desire a friendship or romantic relationship with an attractive confederate by having that confederate indicate an interest in and eagerness to form new relationships at college. For those assigned to the exchange condition, the same confederate conveyed that he or she was married, busy, and uninterested in forming new relationships.

Participants in these studies reacted positively to the confederate's behaviors that conformed to exchange rules if they had been led to desire an exchange relationship. They reacted negatively to exactly the same behaviors if they had been led to desire a communal relationship. For instance, after helping a confederate, students led to desire an exchange relationship with her liked her better if she repaid them than if she did not. In contrast, those led to desire a communal relationship liked the confederate more if she did not repay than if she did repay (Clark and Mills, 1979). Like repayments, requests for repayments of favors done also elicited increased liking when an exchange relationship was desired, but decreased liking when a communal relationship was desired (Clark and Mills, 1979). Finally, people having or desiring exchange relationships were found to keep track of individual inputs into joint tasks for which there would be rewards (Clark, 1984; Clark, Mills, and Corcoran, 1989). People having or desiring communal relationships did not, and sometimes even bent over backwards to avoid keeping track of such inputs (Clark, 1984). Presumably, avoidance of record keeping is a signal to the other that one desires a communal relationship.

Adherence to communal norms occurs more frequently (and is reacted to more positively) in certain relationships than in others. Later experimental studies showed that people led to desire a communal relationship behave in more helpful ways and respond more positively to a confederate's noncontingent, supportive behaviors and bids for help than do those led to desire an exchange relationship. For instance, those led to desire a communal rather than an exchange relationship were more likely to keep track of the other's needs (Clark, Mills, and Corcoran, 1989; Clark, Mills, and Powell, 1986), help the other (Clark, Ouellette, Powell, and Milberg, 1987), and respond positively to the other's expression of emotion (Clark and Taraban, 1991). They also were more likely to show improvements in their moods after having helped their partners (Williamson and Clark, 1989, 1992) and drops in moods after having refused requests for help (Williamson, Pegalis, Behan, and Clark, 1996). Those led to desire communal relationships also are more likely to monitor whether the other keeps track of their needs than were those led to desire exchange relationships (Clark, Dubash, and Mills, 1998).

Finally, it has been shown that people in exchange relationships may respond negatively to communal behaviors or expectations on the other's part. For instance, when exchange, but not communal, relationships are desired, another person's expression of sadness reduces liking for that person (Clark and Taraban, 1991), and choosing to help the other can cause moods to drop (Williamson and Clark, 1989, 1992). It also is notable that when exchange relationships are desired, refusing to help one's partner actually results in improvements in moods (Williamson and others, 1996).

A Quantitative Dimension of Communal Relationships. Although work on communal and exchange relationships began with a qualitative distinction, Clark and Mills (1993; Mills and Clark, 1982) soon pointed out that there is a quantitative dimension of strength to communal relationships as well. Communal strength refers to the degree of responsibility for another person's welfare that a relationship partner assumes.

Some communal relationships are very strong. In such relationships, the person feels tremendous responsibility for the partner's welfare and goes to great costs in terms of money, time, and self-sacrifice to benefit the other in response to the other's needs. Most parents' relationships with their children exemplify very strong communal relationships.

In weaker communal relationships, people take on less responsibility for one another's welfare and incur fewer costs to benefit the other. People who describe one another as friends, for instance, take on some responsibility for one another's welfare, but it tends to be far less than that they assume for their children. Still other communal relationships are very weak. Members of such relationships meet each other's needs only when the cost is quite small. For instance, neighbors might take in a person's mail and strangers might tell one another the time on a noncontingent basis, but that is about all.

The qualitative distinction between communal and exchange relationships and the quantitative dimension of communal relationships are depicted in Figure 1.1. The strength of one hypothetical person's communal relationships is depicted along the x-axis and runs from weak to very strong communal relationships. The degree of cost that a person is willing to incur to benefit a partner is depicted along the y-axis and runs from low to high. The dotted line running diagonally through the graph depicts an implicit boundary line. It splits situations according to whether a communal norm will be seen as appropriate. Situations falling below the line are those in which adherence to communal norms is appropriate. Situations falling above the line are those in which benefits will not be given or will be given on a noncommunal basis (for example, on an exchange basis).

Imagine, for instance, a person's interactions with her best friend. Within moderate cost boundaries, she does lots of things for that friend on a communal basis. She takes the friend to lunch, listens to her emotional concerns, and buys her a birthday present, and she pays for her own plane flight to attend her friend's wedding. However, she does not consider providing her friend with a house, car, or college tuition. These benefits cross the cost line, which is shown explicitly in Figure 1.1 and felt implicitly in relationships.

As Figure 1.1 makes clear, it is possible to have both a communal and exchange relationship with the same partner, dependent on the costs

Figure 1.1. Application of Communal Norms as a Function of the Communal Strength of a Relationship and the Cost of Benefits

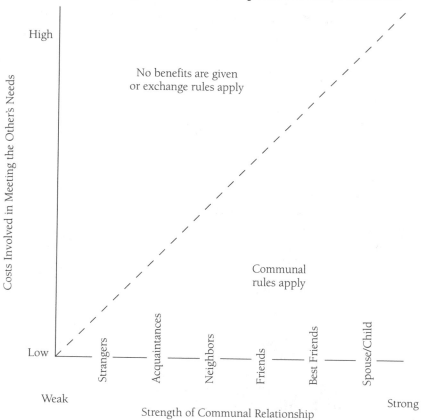

Note: Placement of relationships along the x-axis is for illustrative purposes only. The ordering of types of relationships will vary between individuals.

involved in providing benefits. (Note that the order of relationships along the x-axis and the exact shape and height of the implicit boundary line determining when communal norms are applicable will vary among persons.)

Communal relationships can be symmetrical or asymmetrical in terms of the degree of responsibility members assume for one another. Friendships and romantic relationships tend to be symmetrical, with members assuming the equivalent degrees of responsibility. Parent-child relationships (especially with young children) tend to be asymmetrical. Parents assume far more responsibility for the needs of the child than vice versa.

What the Distinction Is Not. The distinction between communal and other relationships is not one between long-term and short-term relationships (Clark and Mills, 1993). A communal relationship can have a short or long duration. For instance, a person might inform a stranger of the time on a communal basis. Friendships, family relationships, and marriages, in contrast, often operate on a communal basis for years. Exchange relationships also may be short or long term. Cab drivers have short exchange relationships with passengers. Employers often have long exchange relationships with employees.

The distinction between communal and other relationships also is not one between altruistic and nonaltruistic relationships. People can be motivated to adopt a communal norm for relatively selfish or relatively unselfish motives. A relatively unselfish motive for adopting a communal norm is empathy with another's plight. A relatively selfish motive for adopting a communal norm is a desire to form new friendships because one is lonely. People also may be motivated to follow an exchange norm, again for relatively selfish or unselfish reasons. A selfish motive for adopting an exchange norm with a store owner is that one wishes to acquire a particular product. A relatively unselfish motive for following an exchange norm is that one does not wish to exploit a person who has been the source of benefits.

Recent Theorizing and Empirical Work

Our initial empirical work focused on demonstrating that communal norms were distinct from exchange norms and that adherence to each was dependent on relationship context. In early work, we made no distinction between norms judged to be ideal for a particular type of relationship and day-to-day adherence to the norms.

More recently, we have distinguished between norms that are considered ideal for purposes of giving and receiving benefits in relationships such as marriage and friendships, and actual day-to-day behavior within these relationships (Clark and Chrisman, 1994; Clark and Grote, 1998; Grote and Clark, 1998; Clark, Graham, and Grote, forthcoming). More specifically, we focused on normatively strong communal relationships, such as marriages, dating relationships, and close friendships. We asked: Do people believe that communal norms are ideal for these relationships? If so, what predicts people's ability to live up to communal norms? What happens when they fail to adhere to communal norms in these relationships? Is failure to adhere to communal norms harmful to these relationships?

Preference for Communal Norms in Close Relationships. Recent research supports the notion that within Western culture, following communal norms is perceived to be best for marriages, dating relationships, and friendships. When members of married couples were presented with prototypes of communal, exchange, equity, and equality norms and were asked which norms are ideal for their marriages, they overwhelmingly endorsed a communal norm. This occurred whether they were asked shortly prior to marriage, two years later, or twenty years later (Grote and Clark, 1998; Clark, Graham, and Grote, forthcoming). Exchange and equity norms were considered not at all ideal, and ratings of an equality norm fell either between those for a communal norm and exchange and equity norms (for younger respondents) or close to ratings of exchange and equity norms (for older respondents). Similar findings were obtained for college students who rated norms for dating relationships and friendships (Clark and Grote, 2001).

Why is a communal norm considered ideal for marriages, dating relationships, and friendships? The easiest answer is to explain what is wrong with alternative norms.

First, consider the possibility of each person acting in a self-interested manner. This approach individuates persons and carries no implications that one person cares for the other. A person who needs help is responsible for finding it. Thus, felt security should be low. Furthermore, a person who gives help only for self-interested reasons is not afforded a sense of nurturing his or her partner. Without having a sense of mutual caring, feelings of intimacy, as Reis and Shaver (1988) define the term, should be low. To make matters worse, adherence to a self-interest rule allows for exploitation. Persons with more power, perhaps because they have more attractive relationship alternatives, are in a position to demand that partners be more responsive to their needs than they are to the partners' needs.

Of course, one may ask why achieving a sense of ongoing caring, nurturance, intimacy, and security within a relationship is important. The answer is that these are the things that make a relationship a safe haven (Collins and Feeney, 2000) and provide people with an ongoing sense of social support (Cohen and Syme, 1985; Cutrona, Suhr, and MacFarlane, 1990). Having a trusting, caring relationship with another also frees a person from feeling too great a need to be self-concerned or self-focused, because someone else is looking after that person. In good times, each partner can focus on the other and reach out and strive toward new goals. In bad times, each partner can retreat to the safe haven of the relationship for comfort and care. In both situations, a communally based relationship should be calming and thus should promote mental and physical health.

What about adhering to an exchange, equity, or equality rule in friendships, romantic relationships, and marriage? Is doing so better than self-interest? Is doing so as good as adhering to a communal norm? Adherence to any of these norms is better than simply pursuing self-interest because each rules out exploitation. At the same time, adherence to these norms cannot provide the same sense of nurturance, being cared for, and security as can adherence to a communal norm because in each case, benefits are given and accepted contingently.

Not only does adherence to a communal norm prevent exploitation and provide security, but it is cognitively feasible to attend to a partner's needs and strive to meet them. In contrast, competently following norms such as exchange, equity, or equality seems to us to be a cognitively overwhelming task. People who interact frequently, in varied domains and over time, give and receive many diverse benefits. It would be extremely effortful even to try to keep careful track of them all as they occur and accumulate. Beyond that, balancing them according to an exchange, equity, or equality rule requires placing them all on the same value scale before computing equity, equality, or the equivalence of specific exchanges. These are calculations that, we believe, people simply cannot do and, in the best of circumstances, do not even attempt to do.

Applying Communal Norms in Close Relationships. It is not surprising that communal norms are considered ideal for friendships, dating relationships, and marital relationships. However, one might ask whether it is truly realistic to expect that people will attend to one another's needs in these relationships and respond to those needs.

Evidence collected by Clark, Graham, and Grote (forthcoming) suggests that at least in marriages, people do perceive communal norms to be realistic (albeit less realistic than they are ideal) and, importantly, as more realistic than norms such as exchange, equity, or equality. Couples, both just prior to marriage and approximately two years after marriage, report that both they and their spouse actively strive to adhere to a communal norm in their relationship. Not only that, but unlike other sorts of costs of being married, costs incurred in meeting one's spouse's needs are associated with higher marital satisfaction (Clark and Grote, 1998). Finally, even twenty years into marriages, both husbands and wives report that a communal norm is a reasonable norm to follow in practice (Clark, Graham, and Grote, forthcoming). We also have collected evidence that college students report that following communal norms is more realistic than following exchange, equity, or equality norms in friendships and dating relationships (Clark and Grote, 2001).

Skills and Fortitudes Necessary for Communal Norms. There are at least two distinct sets of social skills and fortitudes necessary for following a communal norm effectively. One allows for responding to one's partner's needs effectively and the other for eliciting a partner's attention to one's own needs.

Skills and fortitudes necessary to respond effectively to a partner's needs include having the ability to draw out one's partner's worries and emotional states (Miller, Berg, and Archer, 1983; Purvis, Dabbs, and Hopper, 1984) and empathic accuracy (Ickes, 1993). Many studies support the idea that understanding a spouse's thoughts, beliefs, and feelings is linked with good marital adjustment (Christensen and Wallace, 1976; Noller, 1980, 1981; Guthrie and Noller, 1988; Gottman and Porterfield, 1981). Another skill important to meeting a partner's needs is knowing when and how to offer help such that it will not threaten the potential recipient's self-esteem or make the potential recipient feel indebted, and will be accepted.

Some of these abilities require learning, practice, and intelligence (for example, the ability to draw a partner out, empathic accuracy, and the provision of emotional support). The keys to others may lie more in emotional fortitudes. A person may wish to express empathy or offer help but fail to do so out of fear of appearing awkward or being rejected. One's history of personal relationships in general and one's history within a particular relationship provide explanations for a lack of emotional fortitude in providing help. If one's past partners (or current partner) have not been open to accepting, then the person is likely to be reluctant to offer care. A lack of fortitude may also stem from temporary factors. People who are stressed or in a bad mood may not feel they have the energy to help or may be especially likely to anticipate that negative outcomes will be associated with helping (Clark and Waddell, 1983).

Next, consider skills and fortitudes necessary for eliciting needed support from one's partner. In this regard, freely expressing one's own need states to the partner through self-disclosure and emotional expression should be important. After all, a partner cannot respond to needs without knowing what they are. Given this, it is not surprising that self-disclosure has been found to increase positive affect (Vittengl and Holt, 2000) and liking (Collins and Miller, 1994) and satisfaction in dating relationships (Fitzpatrick and Sollie, 1999), marriages (Meeks, Hendrick, and Hendrick, 1998), and sibling relationships (Howe and others, 2000). Of course, one ought also to be able to ask outright for help and accept it when it is offered. Perhaps less obvious, possessing the ability to say no to requests that interfere with one's needs ought to be crucial to the partner's attentiveness and responsiveness. It should also be important that over time, one demonstrates that one does not exaggerate needs or constantly seek help when it is not needed (Mills and Clark, 1986). This understanding ought to increase a partner's sense that the other is appropriately, and not overly, dependent on him or her.

Although help-seeking skills might seem easy, they require certain emotional fortitudes to enact. In particular, exercising all these skills probably requires having the sense that one's partner truly cares for one and will indeed meet one's needs to the best of his or her ability. Otherwise, self-disclosure, emotional expression, and asking for help seem inadvisable. Under such circumstances, one risks being rebuffed or rejected, or evaluated negatively. The partner may even use information to mock or exploit one. Negative assertion on one's own behalf may also be frightening, as it too may provide a basis for rejection. Thus, it may seem best not to seek help and not to assert oneself. However, in that case, keeping the relationship on a communal basis becomes difficult. For just these reasons, we believe a sense of trust and security in relationships is key to following communal norms.

Giving and Receiving Benefits in Close Relationships. If all goes well, members of relationships who believe a communal norm is ideal for that relationship strive to adhere to that ideal—sometimes succeeding and sometimes failing, but even in the face of failure not losing faith in the value of the effort. However, this is not the only pattern of norm use found in marriages, friendships, and dating relationships.

In a second possible pattern, partners strive to adhere to a communal norm over time, but that striving is punctuated by repeated lapses into exchange norms or self-interest, followed by a return to communal norms. The lapses may result when a person's needs are unmet and resulting feelings that to get something from the partner, the relationship must operate on an exchange basis. Alternatively, a person's lapses may result from the person's own failing to meet the partner's needs, fearing that the partner will abandon communal norms and defensively abandoning those norms first. Returns may be triggered by those stresses passing, finding exchange norms too unwieldy, and a resurfacing underlying belief that communal norms are best for the relationship.

A third possible pattern may begin with efforts to live up to communal norms, followed by a more permanent falling away from communal norms in reaction to stressors. Adherence to exchange norms or self-interest follows. This may occur when stresses do not pass or when persons do not have very strong underlying beliefs that communal norms are realistic. Ultimately, if strong barriers to leaving the relationship are not present, such partners may terminate the relationship. In the face of strong barriers, the partners may stay together, albeit unhappily.

Who Will Follow Which Pattern? Predicting which pattern members of a relationship will follow is tricky, but we can speculate on factors that put relationship partners at risk for abandoning a communal norm. One factor is how well one's partner objectively meets one's needs. In a mutual communal relationship, should a partner repeatedly fail to meet the legitimate needs of the other without good excuses, then the other has good reasons not to trust the partner and good reason to switch to contingent norms, watching out for the self, or leaving the relationship altogether.

A second set of relevant factors includes the individual personality traits people bring to the relationship. People with certain personality traits may be more likely than others to perceive that their needs have been neglected and to react by abandoning efforts to adhere to communal norms. Chronic differences in interpersonal trust as captured in the concept of differences in attachment styles (Hazan and Shaver, 1987; Simpson and Rholes, 1998) or in the notion of individual differences in communal orientation (Clark, Ouellette, Powell, and Milberg, 1987) ought to be crucial in this regard. Those who trust that others are good and are concerned about their needs ought to be comfortable adopting and adhering to communal norms and resilient in the face of violations of such norms.

The third set of factors that may predict what pattern relationship partners follow are individual differences in tendencies to use relationship-protecting interpersonal processes. People who tend to relate their partner's faults to virtues (Murray and Holmes, 1993, 1999) and hold positive illusions about their partner (Murray and Holmes, 1997; Murray, Holmes, and Griffin, 1996) may be buffered against abandoning communal strivings when faced with evidence that a partner has neglected one or more of their needs.

Empirical Evidence for Our Model

A straightforward implication of our theorizing is that adherence to contingent record-keeping norms ought to be negatively correlated with relationship satisfaction. Two existing studies support this. Murstein, Cerreto, and MacDonald (1977) measured the exchange orientation of one member of a married couple with a scale including items such as, "If I do dishes three times a week, I expect my spouse to do them three times a week." They also administered a marital adjustment scale to research participants. Among both men and women, an exchange orientation toward marriage was negatively correlated with marital adjustment. Later, Buunk and VanYperen (1991) reported similar results. They administered a modified version of the prior exchange orientation scale and a relationship satisfaction measure to spouses. Again, exchange orientation was negatively related to relationship satisfaction. These authors also observed that among people high in exchange orientation (but not among those low in exchange orientation), relationship satisfaction was lower if they also perceived themselves to be either underbenefited or overbenefited relative to their partner.

Of course, these findings do not tell us whether using contingent, record-keeping rules in marriages led to distress, or, as we would predict, whether distress led to use of contingent record-keeping norms. However, a recent longitudinal study of marriages addresses that question (Grote and Clark, 2001). In this study, married couples filled out surveys three times: during the wife's first pregnancy, when the child was about six months old, and when the child was about one year old. Three measures of the perceived fairness of the division of household labor and of marital distress were also collected.

At all points, husbands and wives, when explicitly asked about fairness, agreed that the division of household labor was unfair, with wives performing more work, even when both partners were employed full time. According to our model, such inequities do not necessarily lead to conflicts because they do not necessarily indicate a wife's needs are not being met. Thus, we would not necessarily expect prompted judgments of unfairness to lead to conflict. But we do expect that distress and conflict (which we took as an index of needs not being met) will trigger record keeping and, as a consequence, increased judgments of unfairness.

Supporting these ideas, a path analysis using Time 1 and Time 2 data indicated that conflict at Time 1 predicted significant increases in perceived unfairness at Time 2 (controlling for perceived unfairness at Time 1). Also consistent with our model, perceived unfairness at Time 1 did not predict increases in conflict at Time 2 (controlling for conflict at Time 1). The results are shown in Figure 1.2.

Interestingly, path analyses of the Time 2 and Time 3 data indicated that once conflict led to perceived unfairness (at Time 2), then perceived unfairness predicted later conflict (at Time 3). We suggest this occurred because over the stressful transition to parenthood, at least a portion of these couples switched to noncommunal, contingent, record-keeping standards of household chores. When unfairness became salient, a focus on that unfairness increased conflict.

People can go wrong in relationships not just by following exchange norms (or self-interest) rules in relationships that are, ideally, communal. They can also apply communal norms in relationships that typically are exchange relationships (for example, acquaintanceships and business partners). The literature on adult close relationships suggests that this does occur. People sometimes self-disclose too much and too intimate information about themselves in relationships that, from the perspective of the

Figure 1.2. Standardized Parameters for a Structural Model Predicting Time 2 Perceived Fairness of Division of Housework and Time 2 Marital Conflict

Time 1 - Time 2

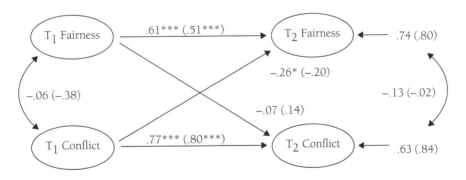

Note: Bidirectional arrows show the correlation between Time 1 predictors or the correlation between the error terms of the Time 2 criterion variables. $n = 178$ wives and 176 husbands. Values not in parentheses are for wives. Values in parentheses are for husbands.

T = time.

$^*p < .05.$

$^{***}p < .001.$

other, are not of sufficient communal strength to justify such disclosure. Liking for such people drops (Kaplan, Firestone, Degnore, and Morre, 1974), and they are often seen as maladjusted (Chaiken and Derlega, 1974). To cite another example, Helgeson (1993; Helgeson and Fritz, 1996) identified a trait called unmitigated communion, which in part refers to persons who are overly concerned with and attentive to partners' needs, sometimes even with nonintimate partners who do not expect or desire a strong communal relationship. Such persons may neglect their own needs and compromise their health.

Acquiring Knowledge of Communal Norms

Developmental differences are evident in the understanding and application of norms. Further, different patterns emerge for communal norms and other norms.

Coming to Understand and Use Communal Norms. The earliest relationship most children experience is that with a parent. Most parents feel a strong communal responsibility for their child and repeatedly (and over many years) respond to that child's needs without expectation of being repaid. Thus, most young children should begin acquiring an understanding of communal rules very early by learning they can count on at least one other's noncontingent responsiveness (Clark, 1984).

Indeed, the basis for the child's first communal relationships may be biological. Human infants are helpless and dependent on others' care to survive. Most developmental psychologists agree that an attachment system has evolved to facilitate such caregiving (Bowlby, 1988; Bugental, 2000). Included in the system are innate behaviors such as crying that communicate needs to the primary caregiver and serve to bring him or her into contact with the infant. The physical ability to seek out the caregiver when distressed serves to keep the caregiver proximal. Caregiver responses to infant distress are also part of the system. When the infant displays distress, caregivers respond with empathy and assistance. For the child, the system provides safety and nurturance. By keeping the child safe and fostering his or her passage to adulthood, the parents ensure that their genes survive (Bugental, 2000).

A second literature that also suggests a biological basis for communal norms concerns empathy. Some researchers suggest that children are born not just with proclivities that allow them to elicit care from adults but also with proclivities toward caring for others (Campos, Campos, and Barrett, 1989; Eisenberg, 1989; Hoffman, 1981). For example, Hoffman (1981, 1984) makes a case that even infants have the capacity to experience empathic distress. They will cry on hearing other infants' cries (Sagi and Hoffman, 1976). Very young children have also been observed to give objects that comfort them (for example, a blanket) to others who are distressed (Hoffman, 1984).

Biological bases for following a norm of care in relationships with others are only a beginning, of course. A fuller understanding of communal norms must await the acquisition of greater cognitive and physical abilities. As the child grows and is able to meet the needs of family members, family members begin expecting just that. Children often are given chores that benefit others (for example, clearing a table, fetching an object). As they perform these chores (with the caveat that they are not paid or bribed for doing so), they learn about the mutual responsibility that is a part of many adult communal relationships.

Of course, there are other important means of acquiring these norms than attachment processes and explicit teaching. Children may learn communal behavior by identifying with or modeling themselves after adults or older children.

As children move out of the home, not only parents but also teachers, religious leaders, and other adults begin explicitly to teach communal rules to those children and expect them to follow these norms. Books and television programs often give instructions about what friendship and family relationships entail and what makes them different from other relationships. It is from such ubiquitous sources that, we believe, virtually all children, regardless of the nature of their early experiences within families, learn the ideal norms for such relationships. In contrast, it is, we suspect, diversity in personal experiences in families of origin (and perhaps in some other early relationships as well) that accounts for differences in abilities and fortitudes to live up to these norms.

Peer relationships also should be important contexts for learning about communal norms. Early friendships are based largely on proximity and similarity rather than on mutual communal orientation (Selman, 1980). Nonetheless, early friendships provide contexts in which children learn to meet others' needs noncontingently. Parents, teachers, and guidance counselors are likely to urge their children to attend to friends' needs and desires. Moreover, peers themselves selectively play with others who meet their needs, thereby reinforcing communal behaviors.

Still, communal relationships do not exist in their adult form until children internalize communal norms and become adept at inferring others' needs and acting in responsive ways based on their understanding and acceptance of those needs (Reis and Shaver, 1988; Reis and Patrick, 1996). This requires perspective-taking skills that do not emerge until at least preadolescence and explains why it is not until children are eleven or twelve years old that their friendships fit the adult definition of such a relationship. Children at this age become close to a few peers to whom they self-disclose and feel intimate, while they remain friendly with a larger group of peers. Among a group of intimates, members infer and meet one another's needs based on mutual understandings. This fits with Diaz and Berndt's (1982) report that eighth graders know their friends much better (in terms of the intimate details of their lives) than do fourth graders and with Damon's (1983) finding that although young children define their relationships in terms of similarities or the number of interactions they have with others, adolescents say their relationships are grounded in loyalty and intimacy.

Coming to Understand Other Norms. Although parent-child relationships are largely communal, parents also teach their children that other norms apply in other relationships. Parents and other adults teach their children about exchange relationships through example. For instance, parents pay for restaurant meals but not for meals at relatives' homes.

Initially, a very young child cannot explore the concept of exchange norms due to limits on the child's ability to participate directly in an exchange relationship. As the child moves out of the home and begins to use money, he or she learns about exchange relationships through participating in them.

Interactions with peers also contribute to understanding exchange relationships. Whereas relationships with good friends may be largely communal in nature, peers on the edge of friendship networks may behave in accordance with exchange norms. They may be willing to provide benefits to the child only if promised something comparable in return. They are likely to pay little attention to the child's needs, choosing to interact with the child only when they want something and have something to offer in exchange.

Of course, following an exchange norm is not the only alternative means of giving and receiving benefits in relationships. Another possibility is that people simply behave according to self-interest. Children learn this from observing others' interactions, interacting with exploitative peers, and direct teaching.

Different Norms and Different Situations. When do children clearly differentiate between norms and apply them selectively in different relationship contexts? Much of how this is accomplished is implied in what we have already discussed. That is, children are likely to apply norms selectively in the contexts in which they were learned. In addition, receiving consistent care within the family of origin and experiencing consistently good close peer relationships as well as consistent experiences within exchange relationship contexts is likely to result in a greater ability to make clear and appropriate distinctions between situations in which distinct norms apply.

Development of Distributive Justice Norms

A brief overview of empirical research on the development and application of distributive justice norms follows.

Children's Use of Distributive Justice Norms. There is little literature explicitly focusing on the developmental course of the acquisition of distributive justice norms. Most relevant studies are from the 1970s. Authors at that time tended to assume that one rule is used at a time and that rules changed and became more complex as cognitive abilities became more complex. Relationship context was ignored.

Hook (1978), for example, was interested in discovering how children allocate rewards earned jointly with another child. He studied five-, nine-, and thirteen-year-old children who worked on a task, saw another child's completed work on the same task, and were given a joint reward to divide between themselves. The child participant completed 25 percent, 50 percent, or 75 percent of the total work. Five-year-olds kept most of the money for themselves, regardless of work done (self-interest), nine-year-olds gave more money to the person who did more (ordinal equity), and thirteen-year-olds did the same but followed a norm of proportional equity. Hook pointed out that this sequence closely paralleled (and was probably dependent on) children's understanding of proportionality. Other researchers proposed similar sequences. Although the exact stages proposed varied a bit, these researchers all suggested that children used different rules at different stages of development and that progression through the stages was linked to the development of cognitive abilities (see, for instance, Damon, 1975; Enright and others, 1984; Lerner, 1974; Leventhal and Anderson, 1970; Leventhal, Popp, and Sawyer, 1973). In this early work, relationship context was considered irrelevant. Research on children's use of distributive justice norms came to a virtual standstill in the mid-1980s.

More than a decade later, Sigelman and Waitzman (1991) and Pataki, Shapiro, and Clark (1994) suggested that children do consider context when deciding what distributive justice norms to apply, arguing that children must learn to distinguish communal from exchange relationships. Pataki, Shapiro, and Clark (1994) reported a study that focused on first and third graders' use of distributive justice norms when working with a friend and when working with a school acquaintance. Their results suggest that young elementary school students do distinguish communal from other relationships.

In this experiment, first and third graders worked with a peer (a friend or an acquaintance) in searching a picture for hidden objects. Each child was told that the partners would take turns searching for hidden objects and that the pair would receive a reward based on the total number of objects found. Each child expected to be the one to divide the reward. Each child thought the partner had taken the first turn and could see that the partner had found three objects. The experimenter let the child search for objects until he or she had circled five. Then the experimenter gave the child eight tokens (redeemable for stickers) to divide and two envelopes (one for each child) in which to put them.

The results, shown in Figure 1.3, reveal that even first and third graders distinguish friends from acquaintances when making such allocations. In both grades, children were more likely to divide the tokens evenly (as opposed to equitably) if their partner was a friend than if the partner was an acquaintance. In the third grade, the likelihood of dividing equally among friends increased significantly, with no increase in the acquaintance condition. These results show that even young children consider relationship context when distributing benefits. For most first graders and even

Figure 1.3. Percentage of Students Dividing Tokens Equally as a Function of Relationship Type and Grade

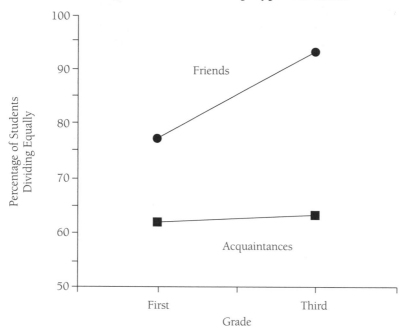

more third graders, their friend's need for stickers was considered equivalent to their own; acquaintances' needs were less likely to be considered.

Applying Communal Norms Effectively. Our focus has been on how children learn and apply the ideal of noncontingent responsiveness to needs in friendships, romantic relationships, and family relationships while simultaneously learning and applying other distributive justice norms in relationships with strangers and acquaintances.

More recently, work with adults has addressed what happens when norms are violated in relationship contexts that most people believe should be communal. Do people shift to self-interest or exchange norms? Might there be individual differences in people's propensity to do this? A focus on issues such as this leads us to consider a wider developmental literature. We are particularly interested in literature that hints who may be especially adept at following communal norms within relationships for which most people judge them to be ideal and who may be especially vulnerable to abandoning the use of communal norms in such relationships.

There exists little, if any, developmental literature focusing specifically on the issue of abandoning communal norms in friendships, romantic relationships, or family relationships when one's needs are neglected. Nor is there a developmental literature on the issue of inappropriately applying communal norms in relationships that most people agree ought to be exchange relationships. However, there are extensive developmental literatures on attachment, abuse, prosocial behavior, and child temperament. These literatures provide important guides to the antecedents of effective and appropriate application of communal and contingent record-keeping norms versus ineffective or inappropriate use of such norms.

Consider possible developmental antecedents to being able to apply communal norms effectively to adult relationships. The most obvious relevant literatures in this regard are those on attachment (Ainsworth, Blehar, Waters, and Wall, 1978; Bowlby, 1988; Main, Kaplan, and Cassidy, 1985), prosocial behavior (Eisenberg and Fabes, 1998), and peer relationships (Rubin, Bukowski, and Parker, 1998). Attachment researchers, for instance, have long theorized and have provided ample evidence that having a sensitive, responsive primary caretaker is likely to result in a child who is securely attached. Such a child is presumed to have a positive view of self as worthy of communal care and also positive models of close others as caring and responsive. Surely having (versus lacking) such positive cognitive models must make it easier to express emotions to, self-disclose to, seek help from, and accept help from friends, romantic partners, and family members when such expressions are appropriate. So too does it seem likely that having the cognitive structures associated with secure attachment makes it easier to be responsive to the needs of others (Iannotti and others, 1992; Kestenbaum, Farber, and Sroufe, 1989; Waters, Hay, and Richters, 1986).

Developmentalists in the area of prosocial behavior (which is often synonymous with being noncontingently responsive to another's needs or adherence to communal norm) also provide insights into the antecedents of being especially adept at following communal norms. Eisenberg and Fabes (1998), for instance, note that parents who teach children to cope with their own negative emotions in constructive ways tend to have children who react to others' distress in prosocial ways rather than reacting with distress reactions (Eisenberg and others, 1994). Parental modeling of prosocial behavior promotes such behavior (Rosenhan, 1970; Clary and Miller, 1986), as do direct parental exhortations to be prosocial, especially if the positive emotional consequences of helping are emphasized and children are not forced to help (McGrath, Wilson, and Frassetto, 1995). From our perspective, however, the applicability of this literature for understanding the effective acquisition and application of communal norms is limited by the fact that the recipients of the prosocial behavior in most of these studies are either strangers or people with whom the research participant would be expected to have a weak communal relationship. We do not yet have a clear picture of how children come to be more responsive to some persons' needs than to others, and we do not know if the antecedents of prosocial behavior within weak versus strong communal relationships are different.

Peer relationships also play a large role in children's lives and should be an important arena in which skills in developing and maintaining mutual, equal strength, communal relationships are developed and honed.

Not surprisingly, cooperative, friendly, sociable, and sensitive children are better able to form friendships than others (Coie, Dodge, and Coppotelli, 1982). Disruptiveness, physical aggression, and verbal threats, particularly in the absence of positive social skills, are likely to lead to rejection (Dodge, 1983; Coie and Kupersmidt, 1983). Immature behavior can lead other children to neglect (rather than to reject) a child, which may interfere with that child's developing communal skills by limiting the amount of practice available in friendships (Rubin, Chen, and Hymel, 1993).

Leaving skills at following communal norms aside, and turning to factors that may lead one to be especially likely to abandon strivings toward adherence to communal norms in the face of a partner's neglect of one's needs, leads us to look at the developmental literature in a slightly different way. For instance, consider work on child abuse by Rogosch, Cicchetti, and Aber (1995) and by Rieder and Cicchetti (1989). These researchers provide evidence that early maltreatment may result in neurophysiological changes in children that heighten their later sensitivity to negative affect and negative stimuli, even in situations in which maltreatment is no longer an issue. Maltreated children, just like other children, are likely to learn that a communal norm is ideal for giving and receiving benefits in intimate relationships in adulthood. Moreover, they might strive just as hard as anyone else to follow it. However, might they as a result of their early maltreatment be especially sensitive to a partner's (inevitable) neglect of needs? Might they be among those especially likely to abandon communal norms and move toward contingent record-keeping norms or self-interest in such a circumstance? It seems likely. A similar (and not unrelated) argument can be made with regard to the potential impact of the negative cognitive models of self and others. Attachment researchers have proposed that individuals whose parents have not been consistently responsive to their needs (specifically, insecure children) develop and carry these models with them over time. That is, insecurity ought to predict heightened tendencies to abandon communal norms in the face of real or imagined neglect of one's needs by a partner.

Indeed, perhaps heightened sensitivity and reactivity to neglect of needs (and our hypothesized subsequent abandonment of communal norms) are caused not just by poor parental treatment of children. An early history of rejection by peers may also account for some of it. Fitting with this speculation are observations that rejected children are more disposed than others to interpret ambiguous negative events as evidence of malevolent intent on the part of others (Crick and Dodge, 1994; Dodge and Frame, 1982; Quiggle, Garber, Panak, and Dodge, 1992; Sancilio, Plumert, and Hartup, 1989).

Finally, consider possible antecedents of inappropriate application of communal norms in relationships most people believe ought to be exchange relationships. Here again, the attachment literature seems relevant. Anxious-resistant or anxious-avoidant attachment presumably results from having had primary caretakers who were inconsistent in responding to one's needs as an infant (Ainsworth, Blehar, Waters, and Wall, 1978). This presumably results in children who are not yet ready to give up on counting on others for care but are simultaneously fearful that others will not care about their needs. They react, in part, by being more clingy than other children, and adult attachment researchers suggest that such people are more likely to fall in love at first sight and fall in love more often than others (Hazan and Shaver, 1987). Might these people be especially likely to apply communal norms early and inappropriately in relationships? We think so. Sadly, these same persons, being insecure, might simultaneously be among the first to abandon communal rules in contexts in which they are appropriate if threatened with signs that their needs have been neglected.

Conclusion

We have reviewed theoretical and empirical work on adults' use of communal norms and have speculated on their developmental antecedents. The truth remains, however, that the fields of adult social psychology and social development remain largely separate and that longitudinal studies linking child social behavior to adult social behavior are rare. Much of what we set forth regarding likely links between these two fields is speculative. Moreover, there are aspects of adults' use of distributive justice norms for which there is no completed empirical work with adults, let alone complementary developmental research. Clearly, much work remains to be done.

References

Ainsworth, M.D.S., Blehar, M. C., Waters, E., and Wall, S. *Patterns of Attachment.* Mahwah, N.J.: Erlbaum, 1978.

Bowlby, J. *A Secure Base: Parent-Child Attachment and Healthy Human Development.* New York: Basic Books, 1988.

Bugental, D. B. "Acquisition of the Algorithms of Social Life: A Domain-Based Approach." *Psychological Bulletin,* 2000, *126,* 187–219.

Buunk, B. P., and Van Yperen, N. W. "Referential Comparisons, Relational Comparisons, and Exchange Orientation: Their Relation to Marital Satisfaction." *Personality and Social Psychology Bulletin,* 1991, *17,* 709–717.

Campos, J. J., Campos, R., and Barrett, K. "Emergent Themes in the Study of Emotional Development." *Developmental Psychology,* 1989, *25,* 8–32.

Chaiken, A. L., and Derlega, V. J. "Liking for the Norm-Breaker in Self-Disclosure." *Journal of Personality,* 1974, *42,* 117–129.

Christensen, L., and Wallace, L. "Perceptual Accuracy as a Variable in Marital Adjustment." *Journal of Sex and Marital Therapy,* 1976, *2,* 130–136.

Clark, M. S. "A Distinction Between Two Types of Relationships and Its Implications for Development." In J. C. Masters and K. Yarkin-Levin (eds.), *Boundary Areas in Social and Developmental Psychology.* Orlando, Fla.: Academic Press, 1984.

Clark, M. S., and Chrisman, K. "Resource Allocation in Intimate Relationships: Trying to Make Sense of a Confusing Literature." In M. Lerner and G. Mikula (eds.), *Entitlement and the Affectional Bond: Justice in Close Relationships.* New York: Plenum, 1994.

Clark, M. S., Dubash, P., and Mills, J. "Interest in Another's Consideration of One's Needs." *Journal of Experimental Social Psychology,* 1998, *34,* 246–264.

Clark, M. S., Graham, S., and Grote, N. K. "Bases for Giving Benefits in Marriage: What

Is Ideal? What Is Realistic? What Really Happens?" In P. Noller and J. Feeney (eds.), *Marital Interaction*. Cambridge, England: Cambridge University Press, forthcoming.

Clark, M. S., and Grote, N. K. "Why Don't Relationship Costs Always Predict Lower Relationship Satisfaction?" *Review of Personality and Social Psychology*, 1998, *2*, 2–17.

Clark, M. S., and Grote, N. K. "The Interplay of Relationship Well-Being and Perceptions of Justice in Relationships." Unpublished manuscript, Carnegie Mellon University, 2001.

Clark, M. S., and Mills, J. "Interpersonal Attraction in Exchange and Communal Relationships." *Journal of Personality and Social Psychology*, 1979, *37*, 12–24.

Clark, M. S., and Mills, J. "The Difference Between Communal and Exchange Relationships: What It Is and Is Not." *Personality and Social Psychology Bulletin*, 1993, *19*, 684–691.

Clark, M. S., Mills, J., and Corcoran, D. "Keeping Track of Needs and Inputs of Friends and Strangers." *Personality and Social Psychology Bulletin*, 1989, *15*, 533–542.

Clark, M. S., Mills, J., and Powell, M. "Keeping Track of Needs in Two Types of Relationships." *Journal of Personality and Social Psychology*, 1986, *51*, 333–338.

Clark, M. S., Ouellette, R., Powell, M., and Milberg, S. "Recipient's Mood, Relationship Type, and Helping." *Journal of Personality and Social Psychology*, 1987, *53*, 94–103.

Clark, M. S., and Taraban, C. B. "Reactions to and Willingness to Express Emotion in Two Types of Relationships." *Journal of Experimental Social Psychology*, 1991, *27*, 324–336.

Clark, M. S., and Waddell, B. "Effects of Moods on Thoughts About Helping, Attraction, and Information Acquisition." *Social Psychology Quarterly*, 1983, *46*, 31–35.

Clary, E. G., and Miller, J. "Socialization and Situational Influences on Sustained Altruism." *Child Development*, 1986, *57*, 1358–1369.

Cohen, S., and Syme, S. L. "Issues in the Study and Application of Social Support." In S. Cohen and S. L. Syme (eds.), *Social Support and Health*. Orlando, Fla.: Academic Press, 1985.

Coie, J. D., Dodge, K. A., and Coppotelli, H. "Dimensions and Types of Social Status: A Cross-Age Perspective." *Developmental Psychology*, 1982, *18*, 557–570.

Coie, J. D., and Kupersmidt, J. "A Behavioral Analysis of Emerging Social Status in Boys' Groups." *Child Development*, 1983, *54*, 1400–1416.

Collins, N. L., and Feeney, B. C. "A Safe Haven: An Attachment Theory Perspective on Support Seeking and Caregiving in Intimate Relationships." *Journal of Personality and Social Psychology*, 2000, *78*, 1053–1073.

Collins, N. L., and Miller, L. C. "Self-Disclosure and Liking: A Meta-Analytic View." *Psychological Bulletin*, 1994, *116*, 457–475.

Crick, N. R., and Dodge, K. A. "A Review and Reformulation of Social Information-Processing Mechanisms in Children's Social Adjustment." *Psychological Bulletin*, 1994, *115*, 74–101.

Cutrona, C. E., Suhr, J. A., and MacFarlane, R. "Interpersonal Transactions and the Psychological Sense of Support." In S. Duck and R. C. Silver (eds.), *Personal Relationships and Social Support*. Thousand Oaks, Calif.: Sage, 1990.

Damon, W. "Early Conceptions of Positive Justice as Related to the Development of Logical Operations." *Child Development*, 1975, *46*, 301–312.

Damon, W. *Social and Personality Development*. New York: Norton, 1983.

Diaz, R. M., and Berndt, T. J. "Children's Knowledge of a Best Friend: Fact or Fancy?" *Developmental Psychology*, 1982, *18*, 787–794.

Dodge, K. A. "Behavioral Antecedents of Peer Social Status." *Child Development*, 1983, *54*, 1386–1399.

Dodge, K. A., and Frame, C. M. "Social Cognitive Biases and Deficits in Aggressive Boys." *Child Development*, 1982, *53*, 620–653.

Eisenberg, N. "Empathy and Sympathy." In W. Damon (ed.), *Child Development Today and Tomorrow*. San Francisco: Jossey-Bass, 1989.

Eisenberg, N., and Fabes, R. A. "Prosocial Development." In W. Damon (series ed.) and

N. Eisenberg (vol. ed.), *Handbook of Child Psychology,* Vol. 3: *Social, Emotional, and Personality Development.* New York: Wiley, 1998.

Eisenberg, N., Fabes, R. A., Murphy, B., Karbon, M., Maszk, P., Smith, M., O'Boyle, C., and Suh, K. "The Relations of Emotionality and Regulation to Dispositional and Situational Empathy-Related Responding." *Journal of Personality and Social Psychology,* 1994, *66,* 776–797.

Enright, R. D., Bjerstadt, A., Enright, W. F., Levy, V. M., Lapsley, D. K., Buss, D., Harvell, M., and Zinder, M. "Distributive Justice Development: Cross-Cultural, Contextual, and Longitudinal Evaluations." *Child Development,* 1984, *55,* 1737–1751.

Fitzpatrick, J., and Sollie, D. L. "Influence of Individual and Interpersonal Factors on Satisfaction and Stability in Romantic Relationships." *Personal Relationships,* 1999, *6,* 337–350.

Gottman, J. M., and Porterfield, A. L. "Communicative Competence in the Nonverbal Behavior of Married Couples." *Journal of Marriage and the Family,* 1981, *43,* 817–824.

Grote, N. K., and Clark, M. S. "Distributive Justice Norms and Family Work: What Is Perceived as Ideal, What Is Applied, and What Predicts Perceived Fairness?" *Social Justice Research,* 1998, *11,* 243–269.

Grote, N. K., and Clark, M. S. "Perceiving Unfairness in the Family: Cause or Consequence of Marital Distress?" *Journal of Personality and Social Psychology,* 2001, *80,* 281–293. (Erratum: *Journal of Personality and Social Psychology,* 2001, *80,* 262.)

Guthrie, D. M., and Noller, P. "Married Couples' Perceptions of One Another in Emotional Situations." In P. Noller and M. A. Fitzpatrick (eds.), *Perspectives on Marital Interaction.* Cleveland, Ohio: Multilingual Matters, 1988.

Hazan, C., and Shaver, P. "Romantic Love Conceptualized as an Attachment Process." *Journal of Personality and Social Psychology,* 1987, *52,* 511–524.

Helgeson, V. S. "Implications of Agency and Communion for Patient and Spouse Adjustment to a First Coronary Event." *Journal of Personality and Social Psychology,* 1993, *64,* 807–816.

Helgeson, V., and Fritz, H. "Implications of Communion and Unmitigated Communion for Adolescent Adjustment to Type I Diabetes." *Women's Health: Research on Gender, Behavior, and Policy,* 1996, *2,* 169–194.

Hoffman, M. "Is Altruism Part of Human Nature?" *Journal of Personality and Social Psychology,* 1981, *40,* 121–137.

Hoffman, M. "Maternal Stress and Mother-Child Interaction." *Dissertation Abstracts International,* 1984, *45,* 696.

Hook, J. "The Development of Equity and Logico-Mathematical Thinking." *Child Development,* 1978, *49,* 1035–1044.

Howe, N., Aquan-Assee, J., Bukowski, W. M., Rinaldi, C. M., and Lehoux, P. M. "Sibling Self-Disclosure in Early Adolescence." *Merrill-Palmer Quarterly,* 2000, *46,* 653–671.

Iannotti, R. J., Cummings, E. M., Pierrehumbert, B., Milano, M. J., and Zahn-Wexler, C. "Parental Influences on Prosocial Behavior and Empathy in Early Childhood." In J.M.A.M. Janssens and J.R.M. Gerris (eds.), *Child Rearing: Influences of Prosocial and Moral Development.* Amsterdam: Sets and Zeilinger, 1992.

Ickes, W. "Empathic Accuracy." *Journal of Personality,* 1993, *61,* 587–610.

Kaplan, K. J., Firestone, I. J., Degnore, R., and Morre, M. "Gradients of Attraction as a Function of Disclosure Probe Intimacy and Setting Formality: On Distinguishing Attitude Oscillation from Attitude Change. Study One." *Journal of Personality and Social Psychology,* 1974, *30,* 638–646.

Kestenbaum, R., Farber, E. A., and Sroufe, L. A. "Individual Differences in Empathy Among Preschoolers: Relation to Attachment History." In N. Eisenberg (ed.), *Empathy and Related Emotional Responses.* New Directions for Child Development, no. 44. San Francisco: Jossey-Bass, 1989.

Lane, I. M., and Coon, R. C. "Reward Allocation in Preschool Children." *Child Development,* 1972, *43,* 1382–1389.

Lerner, M. J. "The Justice Motive: 'Equity' and 'Parity' Among Children." *Journal of Personality and Social Psychology,* 1974, *29,* 539–550.

Leventhal, G. S., and Anderson, D. "Self-Interest and the Maintenance of Equity." *Journal of Personality and Social Psychology,* 1970, *15,* 57–62.

Leventhal, G. S., Popp, A. L., and Sawyer, L. "Equity or Equality in Children's Allocation of Reward to Other Persons?" *Child Development,* 1973, *44,* 753–763.

Main, M., Kaplan, N., and Cassidy, J. "Security in Infancy, Childhood, and Adulthood: A Move to the Level of Representation." *Monographs of the Society for Research in Child Development,* 1985, *50* (Serial No. 209), 66–104.

McGrath, M. P., Wilson, S. R., and Frassetto, S. J. "Why Some Forms of Inductive Reasoning Are Better Than Others: Effects of Cognitive Focus, Choice, and Affect on Children's Prosocial Behavior." *Merrill-Palmer Quarterly,* 1995, *41,* 347–360.

Meeks, B. S., Hendrick, S. S., and Hendrick, C. "Communication, Love and Relationship Satisfaction." *Journal of Social and Personal Relationships,* 1998, *15,* 755–773.

Miller, L. C., Berg, J. H., and Archer, R. L. "Openers: Individuals Who Elicit Intimate Self-Disclosure." *Journal of Personality and Social Psychology,* 1983, *44,* 1234–1244.

Mills, J., and Clark, M. S. "Exchange and Communal Relationships." In L. Wheeler (ed.), *Review of Personality and Social Psychology.* Thousand Oaks, Calif.: Sage, 1982.

Mills, J. and Clark, M. S. "Communications That Should Lead to Perceived Exploitation in Communal and Exchange Relationships." *Journal of Social and Clinical Psychology,* 1986, *4,* 225–234.

Murray, S. L., and Holmes, J. G. "Seeing Virtues in Faults: Negativity of the Transformation of Interpersonal Narratives in Close Relationships." *Journal of Personality and Social Psychology,* 1993, *65,* 707–722.

Murray, S. L., and Holmes, J. G. "A Leap of Faith? Positive Illusions in Romantic Relationships." *Personality and Social Psychology Bulletin,* 1997, *23,* 586–604.

Murray, S. L., and Holmes, J. G. "The Mental Ties That Bind: Cognitive Structures That Predict Relationship Resilience." *Journal of Personality and Social Psychology,* 1999, *77,* 1228–1244.

Murray, S. L., Holmes, J. G., and Griffin, D. "The Benefits of Positive Illusions: Idealization and the Construction of Satisfaction in Close Relationships." *Journal of Personality and Social Psychology,* 1996, *70,* 79–98.

Murstein, B. I., Cerreto, M., and MacDonald, M. G. "A Theory and Investigation of the Effect of Exchange-Orientation on Marriage and Friendship." *Journal of Marriage and the Family,* 1977, *39,* 543–548.

Noller, P. "Misunderstandings in Marital Communication: A Study of Couples' Nonverbal Communication." *Journal of Personality and Social Psychology,* 1980, *39,* 1135–1148.

Noller, P. "Gender and Marital Adjustment Level Differences in Decoding Messages from Spouses and Strangers." *Journal of Personality and Social Psychology,* 1981, *41,* 272–278.

Pataki, S., Shapiro, C., and Clark, M. S. "Acquiring Distributive Justice Norms: Effects of Age and Relationship Type." *Journal of Social and Personal Relationships,* 1994, *11,* 427–442.

Purvis, J. A., Dabbs, J. M., and Hopper, C. H. "The 'Opener': Skilled User of Facial Expression and Speech Pattern." *Personality and Social Psychology Bulletin,* 1984, *10,* 61–66.

Quiggle, N., Garber, J., Panak, W., and Dodge, K. A. "Social-Informational Processing in Aggressive and Depressed Children." *Child Development,* 1992, *63,* 1305–1320.

Reis, H. T., and Patrick, B. C. "Attachment and Intimacy: Component Processes." In E. T. Higgins and A. W. Kruglanski (eds.), *Social Psychology: Handbook of Basic Principles.* New York: Guilford Press, 1996.

Reis, H. T., and Shaver, P. "Intimacy as an Interpersonal Process." In S. Duck and D. F. Hay (eds.), *Handbook of Personal Relationships: Theory, Research, and Interventions.* New York: Wiley, 1988.

Rieder, C., and Cicchetti, D. "Organizational Perspective on Cognitive Control

Functioning and Cognitive-Affective Balance in Maltreated Children." *Developmental Psychology*, 1989, *25*, 382–393.

Rogosch, F., Cicchetti, D., and Aber, J. L. "The Role of Child Maltreatment in Early Deviations in Cognitive and Affective Processing Abilities and Later Peer Relationship Problems." *Development and Psychopathology*, 1995, *7*, 591–609.

Rosenhan, D. L. "The Natural Socialization of Altruistic Autonomy." In J. Macaulay and L. Berkowitz (eds.), *Altruism and Helping Behavior*. Orlando, Fla.: Academic Press, 1970.

Rubin, K. H., Bukowski, W., and Parker, J. G. "Peer Interactions, Relationships, and Groups." In W. Damon (series ed.) and N. Eisenberg (vol. ed.), *Handbook of Child Psychology*, Vol. 3: *Social, Emotional, and Personality Development*. New York: Wiley, 1998.

Rubin, K. H., Chen, X., and Hymel, S. "Socioemotional Characteristics of Withdrawn and Aggressive Children." *Merrill-Palmer Quarterly*, 1993, *39*, 518–534.

Sagi, A., and Hoffman, M. L. "Empathic Distress in the Newborn." *Developmental Psychology*, 1976, *12*, 175–176.

Sancilio, F. M., Plumert, J. M., and Hartup, W. W. "Friendship and Aggressiveness as Determinants of Conflict Outcomes in Middle Childhood." *Developmental Psychology*, 1989, *25*, 812–819.

Selman, R. L. *The Growth of Interpersonal Understanding*. Orlando, Fla.: Academic Press, 1980.

Sigelman, C. K., and Waitzman, K. A. "The Development of Distributive Justice Orientations: Contextual Influences on Children's Resource Allocations." *Child Development*, 1991, *62*, 1367–1378.

Simpson, J. A., and Rholes, W. S. *Attachment Theory and Close Relationships*. New York: Guilford Press, 1998.

Simpson, J. A., Rholes, W. S., and Nelligan, J. S. "Support Seeking and Support Giving Within Couples in an Anxiety-Provoking Situation: The Role of Attachment Styles." *Journal of Personality and Social Psychology*, 1992, *62*, 434–446.

Vittengl, J. R., and Holt, C. S. "Getting Acquainted: The Relationship of Self-Disclosure and Social Attraction to Positive Affect." *Journal of Personality and Social Psychology*, 2000, *17*, 53–66.

Waters, E., Hay, D., and Richters, J. "Infant-Parent Attachment and the Origins of Prosocial and Antisocial Behavior." In D. Olweus, J. Block, and M. Radke-Yarrow (eds.), *Development of Antisocial and Prosocial Behavior: Research, Theories, and Issues*. Orlando, Fla.: Academic Press, 1986.

Williamson, G. M., and Clark, M. S. "Providing Help and Desired Relationship Type as Determinants of Changes in Moods and Self-Evaluations." *Journal of Personality and Social Psychology*, 1989, *56*, 722–734.

Williamson, G. M., and Clark, M. S. "Impact of Desired Relationship Type on Affective Reactions to Choosing and Being Required to Help." *Personality and Social Psychology Bulletin*, 1992, *18*, 10–18.

Williamson, G. M., Pegalis, L., Behan, A., and Clark, M. S. "Affective Consequences of Refusing to Help in Communal and Exchange Relationships." *Personality and Social Psychology Bulletin*, 1996, *22*, 34–47.

MARGARET S. CLARK is professor of psychology at Carnegie Mellon University.

SARAH D. JORDAN is an undergraduate student at the University of Pennsylvania.

2

There is evidence that friendships adhere to a unique developmental trajectory in which exchange relationships based on a norm of equality are transformed into communal relationships based on a norm of need.

The Origins of Reciprocity and Social Exchange in Friendships

Brett Laursen, Willard W. Hartup

At birth, infants have no interest in other infants or capacity for interaction with them. Yet within the first two years of life, they come to engage in coordinated activity as well as reciprocal relationships with other youngsters. Positive overtures are given and received, negative (agonistic) overtures are also reciprocated, and certain partners come to be preferred over others—usually those with whom reciprocal social interaction has occurred previously. Coordinated social interactions and partner playmate preferences are gradually evinced across infancy and toddlerhood, accelerating in sophistication during the second year (Brownell, 1990; Howes, 1983). Specific social provisions are attached to them during the preschool years (Gleason, 1999), and eventually, a complex and nuanced meaning system encompasses children's expectations about friends and friendship (Bigelow and LaGaipa, 1975).

In this chapter, we continue efforts to conceptualize the meaning structures that children use in social relations with other children, especially in close relationships with one another. We aim to describe better children's knowledge about friendship relations and how that knowledge changes with age, and then consider the ways these changes map onto changes in the social exchanges that children actually have with their friends.

Our argument builds on the thesis that developmental changes in friendship relations can best be understood using a deep-structure level of analysis (the social meaning or essence of a relationship) and a surface-structure level of analysis (the behaviors involved in social exchanges in

Support for the preparation of this chapter was provided by a grant to Brett Laursen from the U.S. National Institute of Child Health and Human Development (R29 HD33006).

which the individual participates). In earlier writings (Hartup, 1996; Hartup and Stevens, 1997), reciprocity norms were considered to constitute the friendship deep structure from early childhood through old age, whereas the social exchanges occurring between individuals were considered to reflect surface structures that are developmentally labile. Consonant with distinctions made here and elsewhere (Hartup and Laursen, 1991, 1999; Laursen and Bukowski, 1997), we first examine cognitive representations of reciprocity in friendship relations, then consider behavioral manifestations of social exchange in these same relationships, and finally discuss the interplay between these two levels of analysis.

The Ontogeny of Reciprocity and Social Exchange

Our argument begins with the assumption that humans have a strong, innate need to belong that is manifest in a drive to form and maintain lasting, positive, and significant interpersonal relationships (Baumeister and Leary, 1995). We achieve this goal through frequent, pleasant interactions with individuals with whom we have formed stable and enduring bonds of mutual concern. This affiliative need probably has origins in the survival and reproductive benefits that accrue from membership in a group (for instance, securing mates, sharing resources, providing defense, and assisting with child care). The need to belong is not focused on any particular relationship, but it may have provided the impetus for additional evolved mechanisms preparing humans to attend to social signals that aid in the establishment and maintenance of different types of social relationships (Bugental, 2000). These regulatory mechanisms provide algorithms that guide behavior in the discrete social domains of attachment, group coalition, hierarchical power, mating, and reciprocity. Our interests lie in the reciprocity domain because it is here, among peers, that children learn to implement principles of social exchange, manage reciprocal obligations, and negotiate equivalent benefits (Cosmides and Tooby, 1992). Thus, we start from the premise that the general need for affiliation among humans fosters particular predispositions for reciprocity and social exchange in peer relationships.

Our claim is not that relationship categories are cognitively hard-wired but rather that humans are predisposed to understand relationships in certain ways. Over the course of evolutionary history, experiences that satisfied the need to form close relationships probably also encouraged a subsequent predisposition for adaptive algorithms designed to address different relationship functions. Even the very young display an appreciation of reciprocity and social exchange through self-regulating strategies designed to acquire knowledge through cooperation and negotiation (Trevarthen, 1988). These algorithms encourage the propensity to organize relationships into natural categories that draw heavily on social interaction domains.

Relationship cognitions (what is known about them) are consistent with this supposition. There is evidence that deep-level cognitive structures organize relationships into natural categories based on schemas containing scripts that guide social interactions and shape expectations (Baldwin, 1992). Rather than ranking relationships on multiple continuous dimensions such as warmth and companionship, humans spontaneously classify affiliations according to distinct natural categories (Sedikides, Olsen, and Reis, 1993). Four relationship categories have been identified among adults (Fiske, 1992): (1) communal-sharing relationships that involve equal distribution and shared identity, (2) authority-ranked relationships that are hierarchical and characterized by dominance, (3) equality-matched relationships that entail an equitable exchange of benefits, and (4) market-priced relationships that rely on schemes for weighing the subjective utility of resources.

What Is Social Exchange? What Is Reciprocity?

The term *social exchange* is used more consistently in social psychology than in developmental psychology. Social psychologists refer to exchange of resources as the social events most relevant to relationship formation and maintenance. Resources can be anything from attention and approval to food, clothing, and money (Foa, 1973). Interdependence theories generally hold that individuals are attracted to one another when reward-cost ratios (either actual or perceived) involving meaningful resources favor both individuals; exchange processes are extended into mutually dependent relationships when participants increasingly rely on one another as sources of unique benefits. Variations on this theory stress similarity in attitudes, needs, and values, but in each case, relationships are believed to rest on social interactions that involve an exchange of information or meaningful goods, not merely on the opportunity for two individuals to interact (Homans, 1961; Kelley and Thibaut, 1978).

Complicating matters, social psychologists make a critical distinction between two forms of relationships according to the rules of social exchange that govern each (Mills and Clark, 1982): communal relationships, which describe affiliations with friends, family members, and romantic partners, and exchange relationships, which encompass all others. In a communal relationship, participant behavior is oriented toward the welfare of the partner and the relationship. Benefits are distributed according to need; norms governing behavior in close relationships override norms concerning reciprocity in social exchange (Hinde, 1997). In an exchange relationship, participant behavior is guided by reciprocation of benefits received or anticipated. Participants in exchange relationships have no obligation to one another's welfare aside from ensuring that the benefits that accrue from their social exchanges are equivalently distributed.

Developmental psychologists frequently refer to "social exchanges" when they mean "social interaction." Although one might argue that all social interaction involves the exchange of resources, many exchanges are difficult to identify and measure, and many are too trivial to play a role in relationship functioning. In this chapter, we use *social exchange* in a narrow sense, almost always to refer to the construct that derives from interdependence theory. This convention is not especially virtuous. We merely wish to argue that there are developmental changes in the content and meaning of resource exchanges in friendships even though exact equivalence or equity in cost-benefit ratios is rarely necessary to the formation and maintenance of close relationships.

Unfortunately, the term *reciprocity* is not used consistently in the relationships literature either. In everyday English, *reciprocity* means social interaction that involves giving and taking or returning in kind—matched or mutually equivalent exchange or paying back of what one has received. But the word can also mean "inversely related," thus leading most writers to differentiate symmetrical reciprocity (situations in which two individuals make roughly the same contribution to a social exchange or a relationship) from complementary reciprocity (situations in which the contributions of two individuals are not equivalent but are compensatory or complementary).

The meaning structure attached to friendships consists mainly of symmetrical reciprocity; complementary reciprocity does not ordinarily attract children to one another, supply them with common ground, or furnish the equivalence in social power that goes along with friendship and peer relations (Hartup, 1996; Hinde, 1997). Indeed, one can argue that children and their friends enjoy horizontal, or symmetrical, relationships, because the norms governing them usually call for equivalence in rights, privileges, and obligations rather than complementarities. Parent-child relations, in contrast, are good examples of vertical, or complementary, relationships (Reis, Collins, and Berscheid, 2000). Parents give care, and children receive it; parents teach, and children learn; parents supervise, and children are supervised. To be sure, relationships of any kind involve mixtures of symmetrical and complementary exchanges; it is the preponderance of one kind of reciprocity over the other that makes it reasonable to refer to friendships as horizontal (symmetrical) relationships and parent-child relationships as vertical (complementary) ones. Here, then, we deal mainly with the development of the meaning structure as it involves symmetrical reciprocity, not what has sometimes been called the reciprocity of complement (Youniss, 1980).

Although reciprocity may be a defining characteristic of friendships and other social relationships at any age, the construct is both similar and different among children as compared with adults. Both young children and adults use reciprocity norms in interpreting and guiding their social behavior: prosocial reciprocity norms suggesting that people ought to return favors ("Do unto others") and aggressive reciprocity norms that permit retaliation ("An eye for an eye"). Unlike young children, however, older individuals think causally about social relationships in explicit, rule-governed ways, taking into account alternatives to the reciprocity norm (Berndt, 1977).

We argue that the meaning structure underlying children's friendships is always recognizable as reciprocity (insofar as they involve matched contributions), but that the manifestations of this construct differ across childhood and adolescence. Specifically, we argue that the child's notions about the reciprocities involved in friendship change from an emphasis on self-interest, to the matched exchange of material resources, to a matched exchange of emotional and psychological resources, and finally to a need-based exchange that emphasizes mutuality and collective concern (Clark and Mills, 1979; Selman, 1980).

Deep and Surface Levels of Meaning

The terms *deep* and *surface structures* are used here in a manner that is similar to the conventions of linguistics (Chomsky, 1965). Friendship is the prototypical example of a relationship that is assumed to involve the "maximization of benefits to the self through the negotiation of reciprocal exchange with functional equals" (Bugental and Goodnow, 1998, p. 401). The essential meaning of friendship is thus not much more than symmetrical reciprocity except that it is usually expressed between individuals who are similar to one another and not kin. Indeed, empirical studies show that matching social contributions are emphasized in the description of friendship relations at all ages. Self-interest dominates many infant-infant interactions; preschool-age children emphasize concrete reciprocities; adolescents and adults emphasize mutual support, the exchange of confidences, and trust (Bigelow and LaGaipa, 1975; Goodnow and Burns, 1985; Weiss and Lowenthal, 1975). Indeed, when friendship expectations are compared among individuals of different ages, one is struck by the fact that reciprocity norms are mentioned consistently, even though the psychological complexity and organization of ideas used to describe these reciprocities become more elaborate as time goes on (Livesley and Bromley, 1973).

Surface structures (the behaviors and social exchanges occurring between individuals) are framed within the continuities and discontinuities existing over time in this deep-level meaning structure. The interplay between deep and surface structure is difficult to describe, although equilibration (Piaget, [1932] 1965), dialogues within the zone of proximal development (Vygotsky, [1934] 1981), and interiorization (Mead, 1934) represent various theoretical attempts to do so. Surface-level cognitions are manifestations of deep-level cognitions, but there is no necessary one-to-one correspondence between them. As a consequence, relationships between friends generally adhere to prosocial reciprocity norms or equality-matched norms, but there may be considerable variability in the actual social exchanges that occur between friends as a function of context, age, and gender (Laursen and Bukowski, 1997). We contend that deep-level conceptions of friendship reciprocity progress from notions of material equality in temporary affiliations to notions of need satisfaction in semipermanent affiliations; these deep-level changes in friendship conceptions are accompanied by surface-level changes in social exchanges that transform exchange relationships into communal relationships.

Cognitive Representations of Reciprocity in Friendships

In this section, we review the origins of deep-level cognitions concerning friendship reciprocity. Cognitive developmental models are considered first, followed by perspectives grounded in social psychology. According to Damon (1977), children develop distinct mental systems for understanding the social world. Drawing heavily on Piaget and Inhelder's (1969) model of the development of logical structures and Kohlberg's (1969) model of the development of moral understanding, Damon (1977) describes three discrete stages of knowledge about friendship and distributive justice or sharing. During early childhood, friendship conceptions are grounded in play and affirmed with material acts of goodwill. Concepts of justice consist of largely self-serving distribution rules based on arbitrary personal attributes. Between the ages of five and eight, notions of friendship mutuality emerge with an emphasis on responding to needs and desires. Concepts of justice reflect demands for an equal distribution of rewards, which are subsequently modified to encompass a reciprocal exchange of benefits. Between the ages of eight and ten, psychological sharing, trust, and intimacy occupy center stage in constructs of friendship. A need-based distribution principle emerges, which must be balanced against demands for equality and reciprocity. Damon (1977) argues that it is the form of reciprocity that changes with age rather than the amount, and as evidence he cites longitudinal and cross-sectional research that details the gradual transformation of friendship reciprocity from temporary material equality to enduring psychological intimacy.

Selman (1980) proposes that social perspective taking is central to the child's understanding of friendship. Synthesizing Piaget's ([1932] 1965) model of the growth of logical operations and Mead's (1934) model of the development of the self in social relations, Selman (1980) identified five stages of interpersonal understanding in which initial self-centered relationship conceptions give way to distinctions between the self and the other that lead to a system capable of differentiating and coordinating multiple social perspectives. During the undifferentiated stage that encompasses the first years of life and the subjective stage that characterizes the late preschool and early elementary years, friendship is conceptualized in terms of individual benefits. The first notions of reciprocity emerge during the self-reflective stage of middle childhood, when friendships are viewed in terms of equality without commitment or "fair-weather cooperation." The onset of mutual perspective taking during preadolescence marks a major shift in friendship conceptions: intimacy, sharing, and commitment now define the relationship. Finally, during adolescence and young adulthood, friendships are viewed as relationships that evolve and change according to the needs of participants. Selman's (1980) initial findings were subsequently corroborated with open-ended descriptions of friendships indicating that adolescents were more likely than children to attribute motives of equality and mutuality to their friends and to regard loyalty and trust as defining features of the relationship (Berndt, Hawkins, and Hoyle, 1986). Together, these studies suggest that conceptions of friendship progress from that of an ephemeral relationship designed to maximize personal benefits, to a short-term relationship dedicated to equality, and finally to a committed relationship designed to satisfy psychological needs.

Youniss (1980) suggested that concepts of reciprocity originate in friendship symmetries. Synthesizing Piaget's ([1932] 1965) model of reciprocity in peer relationships and Sullivan's (1953) model of the development of intimate relationships, Youniss argues that the equal distribution of power in peer relationships forces children to embrace equality and reciprocity in social interactions. Informal rules for getting along are codified as principles of cooperation and collaboration that provide a foundation for mutual respect and affection. Youniss provides evidence that prior to age eight, children tend to describe friendships in terms of the strict application of direct reciprocity in the service of short-term equality. Between the ages of eight and ten, friendship conceptions emphasize cooperative reciprocity, adjusted according to the needs of participants, in the service of long-term equality. These findings were consistent with those of an earlier study that revealed similar alterations in friendship expectations. Sometime during the late middle childhood years, the view that friends are primarily obligated to provide pleasure and entertainment gives way to the view that friends are primarily obligated to provide assistance and support (Reisman and Shorr, 1978). Thus, concepts of friendship equality emphasizing direct reciprocity are revised to reflect need-based reciprocity.

Two models from social psychology directly address the development of children's understanding of social exchanges and the norms that govern them. According to Graziano (1984), developmental differences in friendship conceptions are driven by changing conceptualizations of relationship commodities and rules. In this view, distinctions between relationship resources emerge gradually (Foa, 1973). Love and service are first differentiated, then goods and status, and finally money and information. Young children's conceptions of friendship are limited by an inability to differentiate among resources, weigh outcomes according to inputs, and assess relationship costs and benefits over time. Graziano (1984) cites evidence that relationship resource distinctions and social interaction rules are gradually internalized such that conceptions of friendship equality are expanded to encompass norms of communality and equity. To cite one example, written descriptions of friendship (Bigelow, 1977; Bigelow and LaGaipa, 1975) confirm a gradual shift in childhood friendship conceptions from a focus on reciprocal rewards to an emphasis on support, intimacy, and trust. This is consistent with the suggestion that concepts of reciprocity are transformed from simple equality algorithms to a more complex system based on participant contributions and needs.

Clark (1984) proposes a two-step sequence in the development of relationship cognitions. First, children learn to distinguish exchange from communal relationships. Second, they learn the different standards and norms that apply to each. Because very young children primarily participate in familial communal relationships, their understanding of exchange relationships is quite limited, and distinctions between relationships do not emerge until children experience peer relationships. Because the norms of exchange relationships do not require sophisticated inference abilities, an advanced appreciation of these affiliations develops early in childhood. Thus, peer relationships are initially premised on principles of equal sharing. Advances in conceptions of indebtedness and obligation, and improvements in the ability to infer motives and needs prompt new relationship conceptualizations. Distinctions between friendships and acquaintanceships emerge. The norm of equity develops during middle childhood and is applied to exchange relationships with peers. The norm of need-based reciprocity develops during preadolescence and is applied to communal relationships with friends. Subsequent empirical research underscores the role that indebtedness plays in the emergence of reciprocity (DeCooke, 1992). When considering obligations to reciprocate assistance, older children were more likely than younger children to rate indebtedness as an important consideration in nonfriend relationships, whereas children of all ages viewed indebtedness as irrelevant in friendships.

In sum, there is considerable agreement on the broad outlines of emerging concepts of friendship reciprocity. The earliest friendships are probably based on selfish principles designed to maximize personal gain, and although some might argue that this is a form of reciprocity if it is recognized by both participants, it is probably the case that the first instances of true reciprocity concern expectations of mutual equality. These views gradually become elaborated to include psychological constructs such as intimacy and affection. As stability and commitment grow in importance, children are better able to put reciprocity into a long-term perspective. Equality gives way to a need-based system of norms as children realize that over time, inputs and outputs are eventually balanced.

Behavioral Manifestations of Social Exchange in Friendships

We contend that deep-level changes in cognitive representations of friendship reciprocity are accompanied by surface-level changes in friendship social exchanges that transform exchange relationships into communal relationships. Age-related distinctions between friendships and acquaintanceships in deep-level conceptualizations should be reflected in surface-level behaviors. In other words, as children grow older, interactions in relationships with friends increasingly should stand apart from interactions in other peer relationships.

The first reciprocal social exchanges between peers occur during the toddler years (Leavitt, Weber, Clark, and McDonnell, 1985). Prompted by mothers to share toys with playmates, children are more likely to be generous with those who previously shared than with those who did not. Spontaneous sharing, however, is not reliably displayed until the preschool years. By this time, there are clear differences in relationships. Boys and girls are more likely to share preferred foods with friends than with nonfriends (Birch and Billman, 1986). Girls but not boys also show a preference for sharing nonpreferred foods with friends. (Some interpret this as evidence that young females have more communal friendships than young males, but one might argue the reverse.) By middle childhood, friends not only share candy and toys more than nonfriends do but, unlike nonfriends, their level of sharing with friends is unaffected by prior sharing (Staub and Sherk, 1970). Friends and nonfriends also differ on other types of social exchange. Friends of all ages are more positive and work better together than nonfriends (Newcomb and Bagwell, 1995). Relative to nonfriend relationships, friendships entail more similarity, liking, equality, closeness, and loyalty, with distinctions between relationships increasing from early childhood to early adolescence. Simply put, there is ample evidence that children practice social exchange with their friends.

Some may find this conclusion difficult to square with that of an oft-cited literature review (Hook and Cook, 1979), which has been mistakenly credited with the contention that children do not practice social exchange. A careful reading of this review, however, reveals no contradiction. Focusing on the development of equity in nonfriend relationships, the authors found that young children tend to allocate rewards and costs according to selfish interests or equality norms, and although a rudimentary form of equity emerges around age six, truly equitable distributions do not emerge until around age twelve (Hook and Cook, 1979). Unlike nonfriends, there is little evidence that strict equity exclusively guides the social exchanges of friends; indeed, the mere prospect of future interaction (and the possibility of a communal relationship) prompts unacquainted children to abandon equity in favor of equality (Graziano, Brody, and Bernstein, 1980). Thus, we conclude that not only do the social exchanges of nonfriends differ from those of friends, but patterns of social exchange in these relationships follow different developmental trajectories.

The conclusion that patterns of social exchange are constrained by relationships finds support in a study of reward allocation under conditions of differing need and effort (McGillicuddy-De Lisi, Watkins, and Vinchur, 1994). Across age groups, friends received more rewards than strangers, but older children were more likely to reward friends on the basis of need and strangers on the basis of productivity, whereas younger children practiced material equality in both relationships. In other words, equality characterized social exchanges with friends and strangers during early childhood, but preadolescents practiced equity with strangers and communality with friends.

In sum, friend and nonfriend relationships during the first years of life resemble exchange relationships in that equality characterizes social exchanges. With age, equality gives way to equity in relationships with nonfriends, changing the nature of social exchanges without changing the nature of the exchange relationship. In contrast, with age, the social exchanges of friends are less likely to be equal and more likely to be tilted in favor of the partner with the greater need, reflecting the change from exchange to communal relationship.

Reconciling Friendship Representations and Behaviors

There is no necessary correspondence between deep levels of friendship reciprocity and surface displays of friendship social exchange. Indeed, strong evidence supports the conclusion that behavior is an unreliable marker of cognitive abilities; typically, performance lags behind competence (Chomsky, 1965; Gelman and Baillargeon, 1983). Thus, friendship interactions usually are of a less mature form than friendship representations. Consider the results of a recent meta-analysis of peer conflict management tactics (Laursen, Finkelstein, and Betts, forthcoming). In hypothetical dilemmas, respondents indicated an overwhelming preference for negotiation, but in actual disagreements, they tended to practice coercion. With age, hypothetical accounts tend to converge on actual behavior, as negotiation comes to be practiced more and advocated less.

What accounts for the apparent discrepancy between friendship concepts and friendship practices? Context is the primary culprit. Social exchanges between friends are especially sensitive to environmental demands and constraints (Hartup and Laursen, 1993). Circumstances can make friends act in a manner that would not otherwise be typical of the relationship. Closed-field settings describe conditions in which participants are not free to come and go as they please. Closed-field settings in general and competitive settings in particular alter characteristic patterns of social exchange. Under laboratory conditions of competition, friends share less than nonfriends do (see Berndt and Perry, 1990, for a review), and friends disagree more and engage in more coercive behavior than nonfriends do (Hartup and others, 1993). It appears that in closed-field competitive circumstances, the rules governing voluntary relationships are temporarily suspended, encouraging friends to act in the same manner as family members (whose future social interactions are assured regardless of behavior). When closed-field conditions are altered such that competition is not required, children behave much as they would in open-field settings. Relative to nonfriends, friends are more likely to maximize relationship gains (Knight and Chao, 1991) and manage conflict in a more constructive manner (Nelson and Aboud, 1985).

This interplay of competition, setting, and relationship was captured in an experimental study of resource distribution in which friends and non-friends were given congruent or incongruent reports as to whether the candy given to one child had been earned or was supposed to be shared (Staub and Noerenberg, 1981). On a subsequent task involving competition for resources, friends were slower to share than nonfriends if both were earlier provided with congruent information about the candy, but friends were quicker to share than nonfriends if the prior discrepant information was the source of a conflict, presumably because the disagreement diminished the salience of the competitive task (and its emphasis on personal gain) and heightened the salience of the relationship (and its emphasis on communal sharing).

Developmental evidence is limited, but two studies provide support for the assertion that older children are better than younger children at matching social exchanges to settings. Unfortunately, both studies were limited to non-friend relationships. In the first study, age differences in allocations were modified by amount of input and type of outcome (Hook, 1982). Under conditions where inputs were unequal, children of all ages allocated more rewards than damages to the person who contributed the least. Under conditions where inputs were equal, younger children allocated more rewards than damages to partners, whereas the reverse was true of older children. In the second study, age differences in allocations were modified by environmental circumstances (Sigelman and Waitzman, 1991). Young children distributed benefits equally, regardless of the situation. In contrast, older children and adolescents assigned voting rights benefits equally, but money earned from labor was assigned according to input, and charitable funds were assigned according to need.

Taken together, these studies suggest that as children grow older, their social exchanges are more sensitive to variations in settings and partners and to the interplay between them. Paradoxically, this may foster incongruence between social exchanges and conceptions of reciprocity, as interactions become less rigidly tied to friendship concepts.

Origins of Reciprocity and Social Exchange in Friendships

We have sketched a model of the development of friendship cognitions and behaviors. We argue that humans are probably born with an innate propensity to understand relationships between equals in terms of reciprocity. The earliest manifestation of this proclivity is found in peer relationships, where participants organize social exchanges in terms of equivalent inputs and benefits. Thus, the earliest friendships are prototypical exchange relationships, defined in thought and deed by material equality. These friendships are transformed across childhood by social interactions and advances in cognitive and perspective taking abilities. By preadolescence, deep-level conceptions of friendship have expanded beyond companionship to include intimacy, trust, and commitment. Surface-level patterns of friendship evince similar changes; play is eclipsed by affection, self-disclosure, and emotional support. There is more surface-level variability in friendship behavior now than there was during earlier periods because social exchanges tend to be tailored to fit the demands of the setting. These friendships are prototypical communal relationships: participants expect reciprocity, and they provide inputs and receive benefits according to need.

References

Baldwin, M. W. "Relational Schemas and the Processing of Social Information." *Psychological Bulletin*, 1992, *112*, 461–484.

Baumeister, R. F., and Leary, M. R. "The Need to Belong: Desire for Interpersonal Attachments as a Fundamental Human Motivation." *Psychological Bulletin*, 1995, *117*, 497–529.

Berndt, T. J. "The Effect of Reciprocity Norms on Moral Judgment and Causal Attribution." *Child Development*, 1977, *48*, 1322–1330.

Berndt, T. J., Hawkins, J. A., and Hoyle, S. G. "Changes in Friendship During a School Year: Effects on Children's and Adolescents' Impressions of Friendship and Sharing with Friends." *Child Development*, 1986, *57*, 1284–1297.

Berndt, T. J., and Perry, T. B. "Distinctive Features and Effects of Early Adolescent Friendships." In R. Montemayor, G. R. Adams, and T. P. Gullotta (eds.), *From Childhood to Adolescence: A Transitional Period?* Thousand Oaks, Calif.: Sage, 1990.

Bigelow, B. J. "Children's Friendship Expectations: A Cognitive Developmental Study." *Child Development*, 1977, *48*, 246–253.

Bigelow, B. J., and LaGaipa, J. J. "Children's Written Descriptions of Friendship: A Multidimensional Analysis." *Developmental Psychology*, 1975, *11*, 857–858.

Birch, L. L., and Billman, J. "Preschool Children's Food Sharing with Friends and Acquaintances." *Child Development*, 1986, *57*, 387–395.

Brownell, C. A. "Peer Social Skills in Toddlers: Competencies and Constraints Illustrated by Same-Age and Mixed-Age Interaction." *Child Development*, 1990, *61*, 838–848.

Bugental, D. B. "Acquisition of the Algorithms of Social Life: A Domain-Based Approach." *Psychological Bulletin*, 2000, *126*, 187–219.

Bugental, D. B., and Goodnow, J. J. "Socialization Processes." In W. Damon (series ed.) and N. Eisenberg (vol. ed.), *Handbook of Child Psychology*, Vol. 3: *Social, Emotional, and Personality Development*. New York: Wiley, 1998.

Chomsky, N. *Aspects of a Theory of Syntax*. Cambridge, Mass.: MIT Press, 1965.

Clark, M. S. "A Distinction Between Two Types of Relationships and Its Implications for Development." In J. C. Masters and K. Yarkin-Levin (eds.), *Boundary Areas in Social and Developmental Psychology*. Orlando, Fla.: Academic Press, 1984.

Clark, M. S., and Mills, J. "Interpersonal Attraction in Exchange and Communal Relationships." *Journal of Personality and Social Psychology*, 1979, *37*, 12–24.

Cosmides, L., and Tooby, J. "Cognitive Adaptations for Social Exchange." In J. H. Barkow, L. Cosmides, and J. Tooby (eds.), *The Adapted Mind: Evolutionary Psychology and the Generation of Culture*. New York: Oxford University Press, 1992.

Damon, W. *The Social World of the Mind*. San Francisco: Jossey-Bass, 1977.

DeCooke, P. A. "Children's Understanding of Indebtedness as a Feature of Reciprocal Help Exchanges Between Peers." *Developmental Psychology*, 1992, *28*, 948–954.

Fiske, A. P. "The Four Elementary Forms of Sociality: Framework for a Unified Theory of Social Relations." *Psychological Review*, 1992, *99*, 689–723.

Foa, U. G. "Interpersonal and Economic Resources." *Science*, 1973, *171*, 345–351.

Gelman, R., and Baillargeon, R. "A Review of Piagetian Concepts." In J. H. Flavell, M. E.

Markman, and P. H. Mussen (eds.), *Handbook of Child Psychology*, Vol. 3: *Cognitive Development*. New York: Wiley, 1983.

Gleason, T. R. "Social Provisions of Real and Imaginary Relationships in Early Childhood." Unpublished doctoral dissertation, University of Minnesota, 1999.

Goodnow, J. J., and Burns, A. *A Child's Eye*. Sydney: Alwin, 1985.

Graziano, W. G. "A Developmental Approach to Social Exchange Processes." In J. C. Masters and K. Yarkin-Levin (eds.), *Boundary Areas in Social and Developmental Psychology*. Orlando, Fla.: Academic Press, 1984.

Graziano, W. G., Brody, G. H., and Bernstein, S. "Effects of Information About Future Interaction and Peer's Motivation on Peer Reward Allocations." *Developmental Psychology*, 1980, *16*, 475–482.

Hartup, W. W. "The Company They Keep: Friendships and Their Developmental Significance." *Child Development*, 1996, *67*, 1–13.

Hartup, W. W., French, D. C., Laursen, B., Johnston, K. M., and Ogawa, J. "Conflict and Friendship Relations in Middle Childhood: Behavior in a Closed-Field Situation." *Child Development*, 1993, *64*, 445–454.

Hartup, W. W., and Laursen, B. "Relationships as Developmental Contexts." In R. Cohen and A. W. Siegel (eds.), *Context and Development*. Mahwah, N.J.: Erlbaum, 1991.

Hartup, W. W., and Laursen, B. "Conflict and Context in Peer Relations." In C. H. Hart (ed.), *Children on Playgrounds: Research Perspectives and Applications*. Albany: State University of New York Press, 1993.

Hartup, W. W., and Laursen, B. "Relationships as Developmental Contexts: Retrospective Themes and Contemporary Issues." In W. A. Collins and B. Laursen (eds.), *The Minnesota Symposia on Child Psychology*, Vol. 30: *Relationships as Developmental Contexts*. Mahwah, N.J.: Erlbaum, 1999.

Hartup, W. W., and Stevens, N. "Friendships and Adaptation in the Life Course." *Psychological Bulletin*, 1997, *121*, 355–370.

Hinde, R. A. *Relationships: A Dialectical Perspective*. Hove, U.K.: Psychology Press, 1997.

Homans, G. C. *Social Behavior: Its Elementary Forms*. New York: Harcourt, 1961.

Hook, J. G. "The Development of Equity and Altruism in Judgments of Reward and Damage Allocation." *Developmental Psychology*, 1982, *18*, 825–834.

Hook, J. G., and Cook, T. D. "Equity Theory and the Cognitive Ability of Children." *Psychological Bulletin*, 1979, *86*, 429–445.

Howes, C. "Patterns of Friendship." *Child Development*, 1983, *54*, 1043–1053.

Kelley, H. H., and Thibaut, J. W. *Interpersonal Relations: A Theory of Interdependence*. New York: Wiley, 1978.

Knight, G. P., and Chao, C. "Cooperative, Competitive, and Individualistic Social Values Among 8- to 12-Year-Old Siblings, Friends, and Acquaintances." *Personality and Social Psychology Bulletin*, 1991, *17*, 201–211.

Kohlberg, L. "Stage and Sequence: The Cognitive-Developmental Approach to Socialization." In D. Goslin (ed.), *Handbook of Socialization Theory and Research*. Skokie, Ill.: Rand McNally, 1969.

Laursen, B., and Bukowski, W. M. "A Developmental Guide to the Organisation of Close Relationships." *International Journal of Behavioral Development*, 1997, *21*, 747–770.

Laursen, B., Finkelstein, B. D., and Betts, N. T. "A Developmental Meta-Analysis of Peer Conflict Resolution." *Developmental Review*, forthcoming.

Leavitt, M. J., Weber, R. A., Clark, M. C., and McDonnell, P. "Reciprocity of Exchange in Toddler Sharing Behavior." *Developmental Psychology*, 1985, *21*, 122–123.

Livesley, W. J., and Bromley, D. B. *Personal Perception in Childhood and Adolescence*. New York: Wiley, 1973.

McGillicuddy-De Lisi, A. V., Watkins, C., and Vinchur, A. J. "The Effect of Relationship on Children's Distributive Justice Reasoning." *Child Development*, 1994, *65*, 1694–1700.

Mead, G. H. *Mind, Self and Society*. Chicago: University of Chicago Press, 1934.

Mills, J., and Clark, M. S. "Exchange and Communal Relationships." In L. Wheeler (ed.), *Review of Personality and Social Psychology*. Thousand Oaks, Calif.: Sage, 1982.

Nelson, J., and Aboud, F. E. "The Resolution of Social Conflict Between Friends." *Child Development*, 1985, *56*, 1009–1017.

Newcomb, A. F., and Bagwell, C. L. "Children's Friendship Relations: A Meta-Analytic Review." *Psychological Bulletin*, 1995, *117*, 306–347.

Piaget, J. *The Moral Judgment of the Child.* New York: Free Press, 1965. (Originally published 1932.)

Piaget, J., and Inhelder, B. *The Psychology of the Child.* New York: Basic Books, 1969.

Reis, H. T., Collins, W. A., and Berscheid, E. "The Relationship Context of Human Behavior and Development." *Psychological Bulletin*, 2000, *126*, 844–872.

Reisman, J. M., and Shorr, S. I. "Friendship Claims and Expectations Among Children and Adults." *Child Development*, 1978, *49*, 913–916.

Sedikides, C., Olsen, N., and Reis, H. T. "Relationships as Natural Categories." *Journal of Personality and Social Psychology*, 1993, *64*, 71–82.

Selman, R. L. *The Growth of Interpersonal Understanding: Developmental and Clinical Analyses.* Orlando, Fla.: Academic Press, 1980.

Sigelman, C. K., and Waitzman, K. A. "The Development of Distributive Justice Orientations: Contextual Influences on Children's Resource Allocations." *Child Development*, 1991, *62*, 1367–1378.

Staub, E., and Noerenberg, H. "Property Rights, Deservingness, Reciprocity, Friendship: The Transactional Character of Children's Sharing Behavior." *Journal of Personality and Social Psychology*, 1981, *40*, 271–289.

Staub, E., and Sherk, L. "Need for Approval, Children's Sharing, and Reciprocity in Sharing." *Child Development*, 1970, *41*, 243–252.

Sullivan, H. S. *The Interpersonal Theory of Psychiatry.* New York: Norton, 1953.

Trevarthen, C. "Universal Cooperative Motives: How Infants Begin to Know the Language and Culture of Their Parents." In G. Jahoda and I. M. Lewis (eds.), *Acquiring Culture: Cross-Cultural Studies in Child Development*. London: Croom Helm, 1988.

Vygotsky, L. S. *Thought and Language.* Cambridge, Mass.: MIT Press, 1981. (Originally published 1934.)

Weiss, L., and Lowenthal, M. F. "Life-Course Perspectives on Friendship." In M. F. Lowenthal, M. Thurnher, and D. Chiriboga (eds.), *Four Stages of Life: A Comparative Study of Women and Men Facing Transitions*. San Francisco: Jossey-Bass, 1975.

Youniss, J. *Parents and Peers in Social Development: A Sullivan-Piaget Perspective.* Chicago: University of Chicago Press, 1980.

BRETT LAURSEN *is professor of psychology at Florida Atlantic University.*

WILLARD W. HARTUP *is emeritus professor of child psychology at the University of Minnesota.*

3

The moral domain theory presented in this chapter proposes that social exchanges form the basis for the child's internalization of sociomoral principles and emerging understanding of morality.

Social Exchange and the Developing Syntax of Moral Orientation

Philip Costanzo

When the editors of this volume asked me to offer a contribution to the examination of social exchange, my first reaction was, Why me? My more than thirty years as a psychologist have been largely spent on efforts to understand how human beings, through developmental time and owing to the influence of socializers, transform the distillates of interpersonal experience into intrapersonal realities and principles of action. How the "outer" becomes the "inner" is another way to put it. Although I had admired and written about the careful and comprehensive examination of the theoretical roots of formal social exchange theory by psychologists such as Thibaut and Kelley and sociologists such as Homans (see Shaw and Costanzo, 1982) and have followed its development through the more recent work on interdependence (Berscheid and Reis, 1998), I had not thought to employ social exchange theory as a model for understanding "outer to inner" transformations in the developmental life course.

Nevertheless, as I pondered this seemingly misdirected invitation, I became more intrigued with the way in which a consideration of the connections between exchange processes and internalization of principle might be illuminating. Indeed, this kind of conceptual marriage is precisely the virtue of pursuing questions at the boundaries of different domains of psychology. The social-developmental psychology boundary was one that I have straddled before. However, in the past, I had kept the boundary region somewhat tightly ordered by the compatible developmental and social approaches to attribution, social cognition, and evaluative thought. When I had considered how relationship structures might enable the development of the internalization of standards and beliefs, my colleagues and I (Putallaz,

Costanzo, and Klein, 1993; Putallaz, Costanzo, and Smith, 1991; Costanzo, 1991) examined the implications of attachment theory for the development of internalized beliefs, values, and social frames of reference. In contrast to social exchange theory as a model for understanding significant events in the ontogeny of relationships, attachment theory appeared to provide a more emotion–true account of significant events in relationship history that ought to affect profoundly how we construe people, evaluate human action, and adopt styles of connection to others contingent on these construals and evaluations. Social exchange theory in its portrayal of interpersonal process did not seem initially to lend itself to a developmental analysis of the interplay between interaction and social cognition. It seemed even more remote from the consideration of the interrelations between interactional process and moral or evaluative internalization. Perhaps this rather dismissive opinion was a product of my simplistic conception of social exchange theory as an interesting and useful but limited approach to human interaction. Its apparent narrowness inhered in its origin in reductionistic self-interest or reinforcement theory models and the tendency of its adherents to speak to the short-term or contemporary maintenance of relationships rather than to the long-term survival of the conceptual and moral products of those relationships.

My newly discovered intrigue at the possibilities of employing social exchange theory as a model for understanding belief, value, and moral internalization led me to alter my initial dismissive opinions and accept the editors' invitation to contribute a chapter to this volume. In doing so, my main focus is on the theoretical and conceptual issues linking primary social exchange relationships to continuity in moral internalization.

Social Exchange, Social Context, and the Concept of Sociomoral Syntax

The notion that relationships are themselves contexts within which social behavior is enacted has been quite cogently presented elsewhere (Hartup and Laursen, 1991). To the extent that this perspective has merit, it seems reasonable to assert that the interactive exchanges that occur within particular relationship contexts are the functional units of these contexts. What renders a relationship a context for behavior is distinguished from those elements that render a spatial or physical array a behavioral context. Relationships are contexts because the very conduct of them can be characterized by rule-governed structures of interaction. The individual participants occupying this rule-governed space are involved in contributing to those exchanges that imply or instantiate rules for interaction. Thus, a relationship context is continuously transformed as new interactive elements and outcomes emerge from exchanges. Consequently, it is very difficult to freeze a relationship in time and characterize its inherent properties.

Classical exchange theorists evidence an intuitive awareness of the changing contextual meanings of relationships. Thibaut and Kelley (1959;

Kelley and Thibaut, 1978) use the concepts of the "given" and "transformation" matrix to describe and model how the structural principles governing a relationship at Time 1 (the given matrix) change as the relationship proceeds to Time 2, then Time 3, and so on. Relationships that are maintained over time are those that continuously update the joint values of the behaviors exchanged by the participants. Although the arguments are less direct and certainly less mathematical than those of Kelley and Thibaut, Homans (1974) makes a similar point about the recursively emergent properties of relationships. For example, one of his primary exchange propositions asserts that the more frequently a particular reciprocal exchange occurs, the less valuable that subsequent exchanges of the same variety become. The point of all of this is that relationships are dynamic systems in which the relative value of different exchanges is quite variable over time, place, developmental era, and type of relationship.

From the standpoint of a developmentalist searching for rules that model the internalization of social norms and moral standards, variability in the meaning of social contextual exchanges is troublesome. A seemingly essential characteristic of moral standards or social norms is their durability. If social exchange processes constitute an important origin of social and moral standards, then there must be stable as well as variable elements of social exchange contexts. Things that change with the transformation of exchange structures over the life of a relationship may be considered exemplars of the same underlying and more-or-less stable normative structures. For example, if one acquires the value of reciprocity through social exchange, the elements that are "traded" interactively could easily vary while the norm of reciprocity remains unchanged. A very young child may exchange smiles and cuddles for parental indulgences, whereas an older child or adolescent may exchange doing chores for material resources or curfew changes. The particular benefits or rewards exchanged will be quite variable as a function of developmental and other exigencies of relationship. However, the normative reciprocity principle is an unchanging latent characteristic of the relationship. More important, this latent normative characteristic of primary exchange relationships serves as a predictor of the magnitude of the individual's bottom-line belief in reciprocity as a requirement of relationships not yet encountered.

In essence, relationship exchanges have both a deep structure and a surface structure. The deep structure refers to the underlying unalterable rule implied by the exchange. The surface structure refers to the particular items exchanged. The deep structure is made up of the contextual aspects of relationships; the surface structure comprises the behavioral units that flow from that context. It is no accident that I employ depth of structure to illustrate the relation between the stable and variable aspects of social exchange. The most prominent deep-surface structure distinction is Chomsky's (1957) version of syntactic development in language. But it is a distinction that has since been applied widely, as it was in Harman's (1998) work concerning the similarity of morality to syntactic structures in language.

A few elements shared by Chomsky's original distinctions and those I employ here are crucial. First, developmentally emergent adult-child exchanges expose child participants in the interaction to a social syntax. That is, the interactions come to possess a stable structure of rules that pertain to multiple surface exchanges. Second, the deep structure contains the elements of social or moral competence, whereas the surface structure indexes social or moral performance. The linguistics version of this competence–performance distinction is employed to account for cases in which individuals intuitively know the syntax but fail to evidence it in their speech. Chomsky and his associates attribute the invariance of the deep structure (irrespective of surface variation) to their assumption of the innate nature of linguistic syntax. In the social world, I would argue not for innate deep structures but rather for early initial origins. Naive moral philosophies and beliefs are the elements of interior competence that drive interpersonal exchanges. In the same way that a syntactically errored linguistic performance does not constitute a lack of syntactic competence in the speaker, a morally mistaken social performance (such as a lie or indiscretion) does not connote a lack of internalized moral competence. Indeed, the underlying social syntax constituted by moral or social belief is a likely origin of corrective exchanges when morally relevant norms have been violated.

The last point of analogy between a Chomsky-like model of linguistic syntax and the more homely model of sociomoral syntax proposed above concerns the issue of the relative automaticity of the application of deep structure to surface structures. Speakers seldom consciously consult rules of syntax as they exchange utterances in the course of the flow of speech. Similarly, participants in a social exchange do not make overt cognitive reference to the underlying deep structure of social syntax while in the process of interactive exchange. If the overt social exchange violates an underlying principle of either linguistic or social syntax, we intuitively notice the discordance. In the domain of social exchange, this recognition can come in the form of a corrective adjustment in the interaction or in the form of the experience of an interpersonal emotion or, more likely, both.

An example might be derived from some of the propositions and suppositions of classical equity theory (Walster, Walster, and Berscheid, 1973). That theory presumes that equity (or the principle that one's inputs to a relationship should approximate outcomes from that relationship) is an internalized norm of social exchange—a social syntactic principle. The theory goes on to propose that because individuals encounter punishment for behaving inequitably, punishment becomes associated with inequity during the socialization process, and it comes to function as a quasi–automatic internalized norm. To this, I would add that along with the punishments accompanying inequity, the individual is also exposed to multiple social exchanges exemplifying the affirmative enactment of equity as a condition of relationship maintenance and an intrinsic component of fairness. The cumulative product of these diverse exchanges is an internalized and automatically triggered sociomoral principle of equity.

This principle constitutes an implicit barometer through which the confirmation or disconfirmation of the principle or social syntax of equity is experientially and intuitively measured. As equity theory is stated, it proposes two consequences of the violation of what I am referring to as social-syntactic structure. First, inequitable exchanges will occasion emotional arousal such that those parties to the social exchange who unduly benefit will experience guilt, and those who are unduly disadvantaged will experience anger. Second, the emotion experienced following equity violation induces participants who wish to maintain the relationship to generate subsequent exchanges to restore equity (and return the social system to a homeostatic balance between the surface structure of social exchange and the deep structure of the equity principle).

This interactive synchrony is enacted without necessary conscious reference and is exemplary of how internalized sociomoral principles are both established through social exchange and continuously manifested through social exchange. As social participants or members of the linguistic community, we can be metaphorically compared to the naturally musically talented; we discern discordances by ear rather than by calculation or musical scores. For such "ear players," the syntactic structures underlying linguistic, social, or musical performances are automatically accessed and are matched to ongoing performance contexts.

Without such underlying deep structures, there would be little of substance to exchange in social relationships and virtually no way to establish the ultimate value of the behaviors exchanged. Social exchanges are predicated on such principles as equity, reciprocity, mutual trust, honesty, and the sanctity of human life; it is through a history of social exchanges that such principles are instantiated. In a formal sense, there is no ordered language code without syntax, and there similarly is no basis for social exchange without implicit sociomoral principles. Social exchange and moral orientation are transitively bound to one another, and together they constitute the elements comprising human cultural systems.

In summary, I am proposing that one's unique history of social exchange is the developmental architect of individual differences in moral orientation. Although the immediate goals of social exchange might indeed be self-interest and interpersonal mutuality, the long-term developmental consequence of repeated social exchanges with significant socializers and relationship partners is the internalization of a moral syntax. This moral syntax contains implicit construal standards against which contemporary social behaviors of self and others are compared and through which moral choices and interpersonal decisions are mediated. Further exploration of the emergence of sociomoral syntax from social exchange requires a consideration of the nature of moral development, particularly its relation to the role of socialization in moral internalization.

Socialization, Morality, and the Internalization of Sociomoral Guides: Syntax in the Making

The study of moral development, moral internalization, and the social mediation of the emergence of sociomoral cognition has been a protean theoretical battlefield in developmental psychology for the past three decades. There have been two primary perspectives in this domain of study. The first views variations in moral internalization (and therefore the origin of moral cognitive structures) as a consequence of variations in parent-to-child rearing practices. In contrast, the second views variations in moral internalization as flowing from the interplay between developing cognitive maturity and both peer interaction and exposure to secondary socialization agents (such as school and play contexts).

From the first point of view, parents and other significant socializers are seen as the conveyors of social regulations, norms, and social beliefs. The norm induction consequences of parenting vary depending on the manner and intensity with which parents discipline or regulate the behavior of their children. To make a complex story simple, it has been most frequently proposed and found that warm but firm (or authoritative) parenting promotes internalization of the norms indexed in disciplinary encounters. Overly distant or highly authoritarian parenting impedes internalization by rendering the child's exemplifications of norms externally regulated (specifically, it encourages compliance without internalization). Overly permissive parenting is typically viewed as providing children with independence but little in the way of choate presentation of norms to be internalized (for reviews see Baumrind, 1989; Grusec and Goodnow, 1994; Kuczynski, 1984; Smetana, 1995, 1997; and Costanzo, 1991). Presumably, the strength of a child's moral convictions and the diversity in moral norms among children are emergent properties of parent socialization.

Proponents of the second point of view (such as Damon, 1977; Piaget, [1932] 1965, Colby and Kohlberg, 1987) take the position that authority-based, parent-to-child socialization is an unlikely source of moral internalization regardless of parenting styles because the hierarchical nature of the relationship exposes the child to behavioral standards in an atmosphere of direct or implied constraint. As such, the parental rules governing the behavior of the child operate as part of the outer world, and the constraining forces inherent in the social norms or rules preempt the child's taking intrinsic ownership of those rules through internalization. According to this view, parenting is not insignificant but has its major influence on the child's developing understanding of social conventions and not moral principle. Instead of viewing parental socialization as the source of moral principle and process, peer interaction and the child's exposure to social institutions through education and other media of communication are viewed as the primary social origins of moral thought and belief. For example, in the context of peer interaction, rules are negotiated, exchanges are relatively coequal, and a child can entertain views different from his or her own without immediate authority consequences. Such a widening of perspective through coequal negotiation in peer interaction allows the child to experience a relatively unfettered testing ground for developmentally emergent structures of cognition. Thus, from this second perspective, the dynamic interplay between developing cognitive architecture and process and between explicit and implicit peer negotiation constitutes the primary source of morally internalized principles.

Both perspectives on moral internalization acknowledge its interpersonal origins. Where they differ is in their implicit definitions of the process of moral internalization. Parental socialization theorists characterize moral internalization as the interiorization of external regulations, whereas structural theorists view internalization as the constructed and cognitively mediated product of social interaction exposure in the context of nonhierarchical relationships.

From a social exchange perspective, each viewpoint taken to its implied extreme is implausible. It is implausible to suppose that it is solely parental regulatory interactions that generate an internal moral syntax in children, with subsequent peer interactions constituting largely contexts of application of acquired moral rules. Similarly, it is equally implausible to suppose that the cumulative, frequent, and often intense social exchanges between parent and child bear little relevance to the acquired moral concepts and important moral beliefs of developing children.

An emergent theoretical model that bridges the suppositions of both of the moral development perspectives presented above is social domain theory (Smetana, 1997, 1999; Turiel, 1998, Nucci, 1996). This particular approach to moral development is most compatible with the social exchange model of interactively emergent moral syntactic structures.

There are four major premises of social domain theory. First, different forms of social knowledge (including moral knowledge) are acquired by children through social experience with all relevant social partners (parents, peers, siblings, and teachers). Second, moral acquisition constitutes a unique domain of social knowledge. In Smetana's terms, "Morality pertains to the system of rules that regulates the social interactions and social relationships of individuals within societies, and is based on concepts of welfare (harm), trust, justice and rights" (Smetana, 1999, p. 312). She goes on to define morality as "individuals' prescriptive understanding of how individuals ought to behave towards each other . . . Moral judgments are proposed to be obligatory, universalizable, unalterable, impersonal and determined by criteria other than agreement, consensus, or interpersonal convention" (p. 312).

Third, moral concepts are distinguishable from a variety of other social concepts that emerge from interactions in the domain of social convention. This domain is conceived of as arbitrary, consensual, and crucial for appropriate (but not necessarily moral) social behavior and interaction. The social conventional domain relates to social proclivities that are local rather than universal and are potentially open to reconstruction as a person enters new social contexts and social partnerships. Parenthetically, one might conjecture that social exchange matrices and their transformations over the course of a relationship are the products of the negotiation of social conventions. For example, early in school careers, students interacting with a teacher might establish that talking out in class will be met with negative sanction—not because it is a moral violation but because it is an activity that intrudes on the functioning of the local classroom system. As the student moves into more advanced educational contexts, talking out in class might become a desirable behavior in the local classroom system. In short, the content of social exchange units in the domain of convention is dependent on the needs of a particular relationship system at a particular time, and it is open to change with changes in the system. In contrast, from the standpoint of moral domain theory, moral exchanges and the principles on which they are based transcend time, place, relationship, and the contemporary mandates of variable situations.

Fourth, the internalization of principles in the moral domain is the product of reciprocal exchanges in which the hierarchical or peer structure of role relations is irrelevant. That is, social domain theory, unlike structural moral development theory, does not limit morally relevant social experience to peer relationships alone. Despite the constraining components of authority relationships, they can at times function as arenas of the kind of reciprocal exchange experiences that promote moral internalization. It is also the case that moral domain theory differs from socialization theory by discriminating reciprocal exchange from regulatory or disciplinary exchanges—between parent and child. In essence, in the moral domain, moral concepts are not directly taught or restrictively induced but are experienced by the way in which individuals manifest moral principles in their interaction with one another. In particular, Smetana (1999) targets morally conflicted interactions as a primary source of exposure to the kind of experiences in the moral domain that promote internalization. She notes that "children's experiences as participants in moral conflicts and as victims of or observers of moral transgressions lead to the construction of abstract notions of fair and unfair, right and wrong" (p. 314). Presumably, it is these abstract concepts that inhabit the internal reaches of each individual's moral domain and that generalize across time, culture, and situation. Embellishing the perspective of moral domain theory, I would propose that these exchange-acquired moral concepts are the deep structure or moral syntax underlying social interactions.

The emergence of moral domain theory as a broad and integrative view of moral development over the past two decades allows for a conceptual alliance between the study of moral acquisition and the study of relationship-based exchanges. To the extent that moral concepts are viewed as emergent from the experience of reciprocal interaction, the careful study of the rules of interpersonal exchange as well as the moral rules underlying the enactment of exchange relationships should proceed in tandem, or neither will be well understood by social scientists.

Social Exchange, Moral Internalization, and the Emergence of Sociomoral Syntax: A Speculative Integration

Although moral domain theory promises to advance the level of discourse on the socialization origins of moral systems, it also raises some conceptual contradictions and questions. On the one hand, moral domain theory implies that moral codes are constructed from and internalized in relation to social interactive experiences. Yet on the other hand, it presumes by its very distinction between moral and conventional domains that the areas of content characterizing moral beliefs and concepts are definable independent of particular interactions. Therefore, from the domain perspective, rather than co-constructing moral principles in the course of interaction, participants in significant reciprocal interactions discover preexisting and universal principles of a moral grammar—principles that presumably transcend time, place, and surface social circumstances.

In essence, moral domain theory does not so much propose a universal grammar or syntax of morally internalized principles as a universal semantics of morality. Morality means codes of justice, or psychological or physical harm, or individual rights, or fair distribution of resources. Individuals cannot exchange the abstraction of justice but do exchange superficial psychological and material resources. Similarly, harm is not always directly administered in an interaction but is implied from multiple social exchanges. Here, I do not wish to gainsay moral domain theory but to point out the problems entailed in making a priori distinctions between moral and conventional domains. In many ways, in fact, I agree with domain theory in its portrayal of morality and moral internalization as reducible to a few broad categories of social-relational concepts. However, I would argue that concepts such as justice are as much a part of conventional exchanges as those that are presumed to be intrinsically moral. Indeed, much in the way of direct moral instruction from parent to child involves assigning moral significance to conventional behaviors. For example, instructions to eat with utensils often are not presented to children in terms of rules of social conformity but are instantiated by parental direct and indirect messages that proclaim failure to do so as not "fair" to others and as evidencing lack of caring for the needs of others. Furthermore, such disciplinary exchanges are not usually reciprocal (proposed as a necessary component for moral exchanges by domain theory); instead, they occur through constraining, power-dependence relationships. Is eating with utensils a simple conventional rule, or is it a moral rule? Is it surface structure, or is it deep structure? Is it a semantically narrow behavior, or is it a syntactically broad one? Can we gain an understanding of moral acquisition by borrowing from linguistic models of innate syntax?

Some Closing Speculations on the Grammar of Social Exchange

As morality has been likened to language, so too it may be compared to social exchange.

> Morality is in many ways like language. Both admit of great apparent varia-
> tion. Both appear at first to be group phenomena but are probably best stud-
> ied as instantiated in particular individuals. Both are acquired without explicit
> instruction through appropriate experience of the world. [Harman, 1998, p. 1]

Such similarities between morality and language suggest there may be other similarities. Perhaps, as John Rawls has suggested, morality can be studied in the way that language is studied in linguistics. In fact, linguistics appears to uncover a "universal grammar" behind the surface diversity between languages. Might moral philosophers discover that, behind the sur-face diversity of moral views and customs, there is something like a uni-versal grammar of morality (Harman, 1998)?

Indeed, might social and developmental psychologists discover that same universal grammar of morality through closely observing social exchange pro-cess? To do so, one would need to begin with the proposition that apparently trivial exchanges can be moral exchanges if they follow a particular form of exchange-based grammar; I would refer to this as the grammar of importance. Through social exposure and interactive experience with multiple partners, we come to acquire a set of social-grammatical guides for inferring or intuit-ing the importance of units of exchange. We have several cues to importance, but affect is the most prominent. The degree of negative affect experienced by one or more participants when the surface rules of social exchange are vio-lated is central to moral reference processes. These surface rules of exchange are not universal but are established in the context of particular relationships. Thus, in a particular parent-child relationship, it might be a "fair" exchange for the parent to offer warmth, material rewards, or other authority resources in exchange for a child's compliance with conventional rules (for example, "eat with utensils"). When parental resources are not provided, even when the child complies with a conventional rule, or if they are provided even when the child does not abide by a conventional rule, negative affect will be trig-gered in one or both participants, and, depending on the magnitude of that affect, it can potentially lead to the indexing of a moral syntactic structure on the part of one or both participants. Just as there might exist a syntax of adjective-noun relationships that transcends different surface linguistic forms, there is a moral syntax of importance-to-behavior exchange congruence that transcends particular surface exchanges. As such, individuals are always in a state of readiness to apply rules of moral syntax intuitively to rather common and perhaps banal social exchange. Indeed, such everyday social exchanges constitute the experiential contexts for the manifestation of moral principle.

From this vantage point, no exchange is a trivial one solely reflective of the stage or state of a single relationship. The process of exchange is an overt example of the grammar of morality. We are an interdependent species, not only because we conduct our relationships through the exchange of resources, but because we need interaction with one another to construct, co-construct, and reconstruct the contexts of social life most concordant with the deep structure of our moral core.

References

Baumrind, D. "Rearing Competent Children." In W. Damon (ed.), *Child Development Today and Tomorrow*. San Francisco: Jossey-Bass, 1989.

Berscheid, E., and Reis, H. T. "Attraction and Close Relationships." In D. Gilbert, S. Fiske, and G. Lindzey (eds.), *The Handbook of Social Psychology*. New York: McGraw-Hill, 1998.

Chomsky, N. *Syntactic Structures*. The Hague: Mouton, 1957.

Colby, A., and Kohlberg, K. *The Measurement of Moral Behavior*. New York: Cambridge University Press, 1987.

Costanzo, P. R. "Morals, Mothers, and Memories: The Social Context of Developing Social Cognition." In R. Cohen and A. Siegel (eds.), *Context and Development*. Mahwah, N.J.: Erlbaum, 1991.

Damon, W. *The Social World of the Child*. San Francisco: Jossey-Bass, 1977.

Grusec, J. E., and Goodnow, J. J. "Impact of Parental Discipline Methods on the Child's Internalization of Values: A Reconceptualization of Current Points of View." *Developmental Psychology*, 1994, *30*, 4–19.

Harman, G. "Moral Philosophy and Linguistics." In J. Fodor, J. Keyser, and A. Brand (eds.), *Celebration: An Electronic Festschrift in Honor of Noam Chomsky*. Cambridge, Mass.: MIT Press, 1998.

Hartup, W. W., and Laursen, B. "Relationships as Developmental Contexts." In R. Cohen and A. Siegel (eds.), *Context and Development*. Mahwah, N.J.: Erlbaum, 1991.

Homans, G. *Social Behavior: Its Elementary Forms*. New York: Harcourt, 1974.

Kelley, H. H., and Thibaut, J. W. *Interpersonal Relations: A Theory of Interdependence*. New York: Wiley, 1978.

Kuczynski, L. "Socialization Goals and Mother-Child Interaction: Strategies for Long-Term and Short-Term Compliance." *Developmental Psychology*, 1984, *20*, 1061–1073.

Nucci, L. P. "Morality and Personal Freedom." In E. Reed, E. Turiel, and T. Brown (eds.), *Knowledge and Values*. Mahwah, N.J.: Erlbaum, 1996.

Piaget, J. *The Moral Judgment of the Child*. New York: Free Press, 1965. (Originally published 1932.)

Putallaz, M., Costanzo, P. R., and Klein, T. P. "Parental Childhood Social Experiences and Their Effects on Children's Relationships." In S. Duck (ed.), *Learning About Relationships*. Thousand Oaks, Calif.: Sage, 1993.

Putallaz, M., Costanzo, P. R., and Smith, R. B. "Maternal Recollections of Childhood Peer Relationships: Implications for Their Children's Social Competence." *Journal of Social and Personal Relationships*, 1991, *8*, 403–422.

Shaw, M. E., and Costanzo, P. R. *Theories of Social Psychology*. New York: McGraw-Hill, 1982.

Smetana, J. G. "Parenting Styles and Conceptions of Parental Authority During Adolescence." *Child Development*, 1995, *66*, 299–316.

Smetana, J. G. "Parenting and the Development of Social Knowledge Reconceptualized: A Social Domain Analysis." In J. E. Grusec and L. Kuczynski (eds.), *Parenting and the Internalization of Values*. New York: Wiley, 1997.

Smetana, J. G. "The Role of Parents in Moral Development: A Social Domain Analysis." *Journal of Moral Education*, 1999, *28*, 311–321.

Thibaut, J., and Kelley, H. *The Social Psychology of Groups*. New York: Wiley, 1959.

Turiel, E. "Moral Development." In W. Damon (series ed.) and N. Eisenberg (vol. ed.), *Handbook of Child Psychology,* Vol. 3: *Social, Emotional, and Personality Development.* New York: Wiley, 1998.

Walster, E., Walster, G., and Berscheid, E. "New Directions in Equity Research." *Journal of Personality and Social Psychology,* 1973, *25,* 151–176.

PHILIP COSTANZO is professor of psychology at Duke University.

4

Exchange and development are treated as forms of interdependence and then framed as exemplars of the operation of complex dynamical systems.

Exchange and Development: A Dynamical, Complex Systems Perspective

Reuben M. Baron

I frame this analysis of the relation between exchange and development in ways that depart from the conventional take on both exchange and development. Furthermore, I propose that a new frame can be derived from treating these phenomena as exemplars of the operation of complex dynamical systems (Baron, Amazeen, and Beek, 1994; Kelso, 1995; Nowak and Vallacher, 1998). The emphasis will be on how we get complexity out of simplicity, the importance of focusing on collective levels of organization rather than individual components, and, perhaps most important, how change in general, and development in particular, can be a self-organized activity involving circular causality.

Substantively, the analysis starts with two seemingly radical propositions. First, following Caporael and Baron (1997), I propose that instead of fostering increasing independence, social development actually leads people to become increasingly interdependent with age; that is, people increasingly need to engage in joint activities in order to improve their outcome potential. This proposition is assumed to hold whether one focuses on the role of social factors in general development, the exemplar here being Vygotsky's (1978) demonstration that there is "a range between what the child can do with help (social scaffolding) and what the child can do without help," the so-called zone of proximal development (described by Van Geert, 2000, p. 65), or whether one focuses on social development per se, as in the increase in relationship-building social skills with age, the exemplar here being the child's increasing ability to engage in cooperative behavior, as well as the increasing importance of forming close relationships and joining groups (Harris,

1995).The second proposition goes to the heart of exchange relations by proposing that exchange and communal relationships are systematically interrelated in a developmental and dynamical system sense rather than simply representing diametrically opposed systems of reward allocation, with the former focusing on a tit-for-tat, equity-based principle regarding exchange of benefits (as well as costs in certain situations), whereas the latter, which are typically close relationships as opposed to acquaintanceships, allocate rewards according to need, with no expectation of reciprocity of contribution (Clark and Mills, 1993). I propose that both exchange and communal relationships are forms of interdependence and allocation systems that, at a dynamical level, can be said to be interdependent in that they collectively resemble the cyclical codependence between task and socioemotional orientation that is seen in problem-solving groups (Bales, 1958).

Specifically, in such situations, the output of one phase becomes the input that triggers the appearance of the next phase. For example, during the task phase, interpersonal needs may tend to be ignored. After a while, insensitivity to these needs may get in the way of people accepting certain task-related roles, leading to a period when socioemotional factors get the attention of the group. This interpersonal focus may smooth the way for a more sensitive division of tasks that leads to more effective problem solving. Similarly, it may be that after a while, a tit-for-tat exchange that is satisfying in terms of meeting equity concerns builds a certain level of trust that allows people to be less concerned about equity of contribution and more concerned about the needs of the other people. Stated at a more relational level, a switch from an exchange to a communal orientation may be mediated by a shift from an I to a We level of social functioning. That is, once people are jointly committed to a relationship, the issue of equity of exchange is no longer salient. This, however, may also be phasic. As a relationship is deteriorating, exchange is reinstated as we begin to keep score again (Levinger, 1980).

We can unpack the claim that both exchange and communal systems of allocation involve aspects of interdependence. Consider, for example, the relevance of violating a reciprocity rule in each situation. In the exchange situation, the rule is simple: I help you; you help me. To fail to reciprocate is a form of social cheating. This is but one type of interdependence, one that at a global level involves a tit-for-tat level of relating to another person. There are certain problems with this way of relating. In particular, it requires constant social accounting; we are forever keeping score, perhaps leading to a kind of cognitive overload.

Consider another kind of interdependence—what Sternberg (1987) calls "companionate love." We could reinterpret a communal relationship as fitting this frame in the sense that in a companionate relationship, partners show support and caring for one another in the context of increasing intimacy and commitment (Hatfield, 1988). Writ large, it may be claimed that both exchange and communal relationships reflect interdependence or reciprocity but that reciprocity can become a richer form of relating to another person than calculating comparative input-outcome ratios. That is, exchange relationships may simply be an initial stage of a relationship that becomes communal when monitoring gives way to caring. There is also another model of sensitivity to need—one that expresses interdependence in the sense of Aronson's jigsaw problem-solving model (Aronson and others, 1978). Here, each person's problem-solving resources are incomplete, thereby requiring a cooperative solution. Such cooperation can be seen as another way to view a communal relationship based on still another way to view reciprocity; each person supplies what the other person needs. The problem of interdependence shifts from social accounting to social coordination.

In addition to claiming that both exchange and communal relationships reflect interdependence at a number of levels, it is also proposed that introducing the dynamical view allows a unique prediction regarding the nature of difficulties involved in trying to restore a communal relationship once it has deteriorated into an exchange relationship. The occurrence of hysteresis (Turvey, 1990) is one of a number of unique predictions possible with a dynamical view of development. Specifically, with hysteresis, there is an asymmetry between the level of a parameter that induces a change in state and the level needed to restore that state once it is lost. For example, if a certain reduction in wages resulted in formation of a union, simply restoring the cut will not likely end the union; a larger increase may be required.

Within a dynamical model, a systematic way of framing qualitative changes in a relationship involves what are called "catastrophe flags" (Turvey, 1990). Such flags are indexes of a system that is preparing for a phase transition. For example, if such a system is perturbed, it both exhibits hysteresis and takes a longer time to restore the preexisting state. It is also typical of a dynamical system that as it approaches the transition point from one type of relationship to another, behavior increases in variability. Thus, just before a long-term dating relationship leads to engagement to marry, one or both of the partners may become more emotional, find doubts that delay the engagement, and so on. Finally, in regard to this overview, the implications of the complex-dynamical view for interpreting development will be explored in the context of the importance of self-organization as an approach to development. Here we will explore circular causality, self-organized criticality, and the repeated assembly of basic units of organization as processes of change (Caporael and Baron, 1997).

Development as a Dynamical System

Because I am a social psychologist, I will focus my treatment of development on an aspect of adult development involving the person's ability to enter into successful social relationships outside the family at the level of the dyad and the group. I believe, however, that many of the same principles can be (and have been) used to describe the development of physical-locomotor systems such as walking and reaching (Thelen, 1984), as well as the development of basic social communication competencies involving the coordination of infant movement with adult speech (Green and Gustafson, 1997). In all cases, complexity and order emerge as a product of interactions between simpler local components, be the situation one where the progress from crawling to walking changes the complexity of adult-child communicative exchanges (Green and Gustafson, 1997) or how aggregates are transformed into groups (for instance, the formation of a study group or a hunting pack; Caporael and Baron, 1997). At a microlevel, it will be suggested that social development involves a compression of individual degrees of freedom that is exchanged for the benefits of participating in a molar organization that achieves outcomes impossible at the component level. It is important to note that this dynamical model also suggests that exchange and development are two sides of the same coin; each is rooted in interdependence, whether at the level of part to part, part to whole, or whole to part. Exchange at the metalevel becomes one basic force that triggers and stabilizes or destabilizes the assembly of parts into collective, functional units. For example, the formation of study groups is motivated by the expectation of better grades, the formation of unions by the expectation of better wages (or work conditions), and the formation of intergroup alliances by the belief that the alliance helps the component group better deal with a common threat or achieve a joint goal.

Development in this view involves what Kelso (1995) refers to as the formation of dynamic patterns. In our case, the dynamic patterns involve nested organizations of interdependence, with development adding to the complexity of interdependences as social relations become multiply situated in terms of individuals in dyads, dyads within groups, and groups within organizations. Hierarchically, higher-order organizations limit variability at lower levels, but ideally they remain open to possibilities for change both from without, in terms of external environmental parameters, as well as from the bottom up, in terms of lower-order groupings influencing higher-order collectives (Buss, 1987).

Within this way of modeling development as a form of change, exchange and communal modes of interdependence are constantly reassembled as forms of interdependence as basic to social functioning as ice and fog are to the transformational possibilities of water. And like ice and fog, both are qualitatively different states that lie on a continuum involving continuous variables analogous to the tightness of molecular bonding. The underlying social structural continuum analogous to strength of physical molecular bonding is trust. When trust reaches a certain level, a phase transition occurs to a communal-based relationship, much as ice gives way to fog when the temperature rises. With regard to interdependence, there is a shift from reciprocity, defined in terms of a type of social accounting, to a reciprocity based on a mutual sensitivity to the other's needs.

Another way to describe the communal relationship is as a situation in which local dynamics give way to global dynamics, with the result that reciprocity is now defined in terms of a circular causality. Specifically, interdependence goes from part-to-part interaction to the emergence of a global structure that promotes feedback to modify the parts. The circularity can also take on another loop, as it does with minority influence, when the parts once more influence the whole (see Figure 4.1). Moreover, this second part-to-whole influence cycle (the first is the local interactions that gave rise to the global structure in the first place) may exhibit hysteresis. For example, the strength of social ties among like-minded individuals necessary to change the global structure may be much greater than the local coherence required to produce the group structure in the first place (see Nowak and Vallacher, 1998, for a discussion of coherence as an order parameter).

Viewed in this way, communal relationships involve a much more complex, dynamical pattern of interdependence than exchange relationships do. That is, the ultimate implication of limiting a relationship to an exchange type of interdependence is that the parts function on a highly individualistic basis. The communal relationship moves the dyad nearer to group-based types of interactions, where direct part-part interactions are

Figure 4.1. Dynamical Processes of Change Within and Between Groups

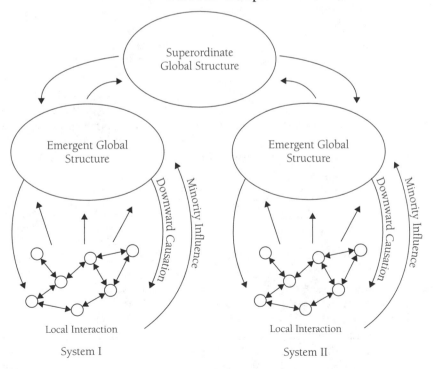

mediated by relationship or group-level role constraints, such as rules for what is proper behavior within the relationship, where proper actions strengthen the coherence of the group (Campbell, 1958).

Interdependence Within a Dynamical System

We are now ready for a specific definition of the developmental problems this dynamical analysis will emphasize. The focus will be on the progressive expansion of people's ability to enter into, maintain, and dissolve relationships of interdependence at the dyadic, group, and intergroup level. A dynamical view implies a specific focus on how a social fractal, the emergence of a plural subject, (Gilbert, 1996), the ability to function at the We level, interpenetrates dyadic, group, and intergroup functioning. We will analyze how "We-ness" is repeatedly reassembled as the core configuration in development and exchange as both a product of interdependence and a determinant of interdependence. For example, the formation and stabilization of a group may rest on ever-changing levels of convergence and disparity between the individual's commitment to the group and the commitment of the group to the individual. The commitment of individuals to group goals makes a group possible; the commitment of the group to individuals determines its stability. In such a view, cohesiveness is a collective description of the state of the group as indexed by the order parameter of commitment disparity (Arrow, McGrath, and Bardahl, 2000; Baron, Amazeen, and Beek, 1994). That is, an order parameter is a quantitative index of the qualitative state of the organization of the system. It approaches one where performance is role appropriate and zero where people refuse or are unable to carry out their roles. In social groups, at issue is whether the right person is in the right role, given the goal structure of the group. In the present frame, commitment disparity would be low, corresponding to a situation where the collective concern for comparing current outcomes with outcomes available in other group situations is low (Thibaut and Kelley, 1959).

Self-Organization

Another critical feature of the dynamical view of interdependence involves treating development as a process of self-organization. Specifically, interdependence in this view involves a system of circular causality where interdependence grows out of local dynamics, as when individually dissatisfied workers learn quite by chance at the cafeteria or local bar that they share certain grievances. These interactions may lead to the formation of a union within which individual workers now function as role occupants whose behavior is regulated by group norms. Self-organization generates circular causality; the subsequent behavior of workers is now influenced by norms and roles (Campbell, 1990). Thus, we make the union, and it makes us (see Figure 4.1). In effect, the I becomes a We, which gives feedback to modify the I. Furthermore, the local dynamics that create the union may also show positive feedback properties, in that the severity of the problems may be amplified as people interact or share grievance stories. Bak (1996) describes this type of positive feedback as self-organized criticality, the effect of which is destabilization. Thus, it is necessary for individual-level dissatisfaction to rise to the point where a group structure can emerge.

Finally, self-organized criticality as a group-level process is proposed to be a mechanism for the formation of intergroup ties, given that tight bonds or high cohesiveness must be broken before bridges can be built to other groups (Granovetter, 1973). In this context, it is predicted that groups that allow minority influence are more likely to enter into positive intergroup relations, given that the existence of a minority may function to loosen intragroup ties. Thus, one may increase intergroup cooperation by amplifying minority influence; the dynamical mechanism of self-organized criticality could be a description of such a process. In effect, the relative strength of majority and minority factions in a group may reach a threshold or tip point. When this occurs, there is a phase transition in which openness to other groups replaces an in-group–out-group framing of intergroup relations. Viewed in this way, low social cohesiveness within a group—weak ties at an intragroup level—increases the likelihood of stronger ties between groups much as weakening a dyadic tie increases the likelihood that people will have a wider circle of friends and acquaintances. In dynamic terms, achieving a higher-order level of interdependence requires symmetry breaking or unfreezing (Lewin, 1947).

Consider a progression of symmetry breaking, a situation in which homeostasis is perturbed. At the individual level, the person, in order to accommodate another person, must both give up certain goals or share other ones (or both). At the group level, individual or dyadic goals are exchanged for group-level goals, values, norms, and roles. Similarly, before groups can reassemble into higher-order coalitions, there must be symmetry breaking at the group level (see the formation of a superordinate structure in Figure 4.1). For example, a community coalition of different ethnic groups to fight drug traffic may not occur even given a common threat unless ties within ethnic groups are weakened. Cries of black power or white power or Chicano power foster intragroup cohesion but work against cooperative interdependence. Finally, to return to the developmental theme of this chapter, consider a situation in which a community organization develops as a superordinate structure. Once this organization is in place, none of the components can function the way they did previously because of a basic self-organizational mode of circular causality. Specifically, the groups made the community organization, and now it shapes them (see the formation of a superordinate structure in Figure 4.1).

A Dynamical View of Development

The idea that parts interact to create wholes that then influence parts is the most general property of both developmental and complex dynamical system ways of framing change. It is the dynamical counterpart of how nested levels of organization continue to grow and influence one another. The nature of such influence occurs at two levels. First, it is accepted that in the course of the development of a system, higher levels of organization limit the expression of variation at the lower level (Buss, 1987). Thus, in our community relations example, once an intergroup council is in effect, the autonomy of the component ethnic groups is limited. However, I would claim that this situation is necessary but not sufficient for effective adaptation to occur in a rapidly changing environment. Rather, it is also necessary for the lower level to influence groups at higher levels of organization. For example, the intergroup community council should not make itself immune to feedback from its constituent groups.

Indeed, the concept of community development should involve exactly this kind of circular causality. This circular causality is a way of viewing interdependence as less a matter of outcome contingency and more an issue of how social organizations—dyadic, group, or intergroup—keep their properties as complex, dynamical systems. Such systems are complex because rather than showing a preference for equilibrium and the elimination of discrepancies from a set point (preference for homeostasis), they exist between order and chaos (Prigogine and Stengers, 1984). For example, in sports, it is necessary to keep a successful team hungry; once one goal is reached, a new one must be waiting in the wings. Thus, one aspect of a complex system is that it is multimodal.

The development of a complex system is not linear and incremental. Special types of independent variables (called control parameters) operate such that small changes can trigger a phase transition, much as a one degree change in temperature can turn rain into sleet. That is, control parameters change smoothly until they pass through a critical point, at which time a qualitative change in phase state is induced. As Baron, Amazeen, and Beek (1994) indicate, Levinger's stage model of relationship development and Moreland and Levine's (1982) model of group socialization embody aspects of change in these terms. Moreover, change in complex, dynamical systems is irreversible. Thus, complex change is risky in many ways; small differences in initial conditions can produce qualitatively different trajectories. And because complex systems are typically self-organized, there is no executive program to turn to for guidance. This optimizes flexibility; rather than trying to foresee specific environmental contingencies and create specific scripts for coping, complex systems are organized to capitalize on changing external and internal environments. For example, allowing a minority faction to exist encourages self-criticism and innovation, the antithesis of groupthink (Janis, 1982).

A Dynamical View of Exchange

Where does exchange enter into such a view of development? Let us take one of the most basic elements of Thibaut and Kelley's (1959) exchange model predictor of change, the Comparison Level of Alternatives. Whatever the absolute level of outcome for partners within a relationship, if there are better outcomes foreseen in some other relationship, the initial relationship of interdependence is destabilized. Typically, this process is treated at an individual level; each partner is going through this type of social comparison of outcomes (Rusbult, 1987).

The first difference from a dynamical perspective is that individual social comparisons are integrated between partners in the local dynamics phase. That is, comparison becomes a collective process; there is, in effect, informational interdependence at this point. Indeed, it is only in a deteriorated relationship that such a process would continue to be individualistic. Out of this local exchange, a collective product is assumed to develop at the relationship level. In such a process, the relationship Comparison Level for Alternatives can be different from the sum of individual Comparison Level of Alternatives. For example, at issue is the implication for the relationship of attractive Comparison Level of Alternatives for the constituents. Note that the problem is little different from trying to predict whether a person who joins a group will stay in that group or switch groups. In this regard, it may be recalled that group cohesiveness increases as the disparity between the individual's commitment to the group and the group's commitment to the individual decreases. The dyad, however, is different from the group in that if one partner defects, the relationship is terminated.

Let us explore some commonalties. First at issue in dyadic or group development is the emergence of a plural subject, or a We level of thinking (Gilbert, 1996). In more conventional terms, the partner's self-concepts become intertwined (Aron, Aron, Tudor, and Nelson, 1991). Perhaps still another way to frame the collective level is to assume that the We orientation takes us out of an exchange relationship and into a communal one. In self-concept terms, if we succumb to a favorable Comparison Level of Alternatives, we are likely to think less of ourselves because we know our partner will be hurt.

Within the dynamical, self-organized system view, what occurs is that the We level of organization feeds back to affect the I. Here, leaving the relationship becomes, in itself, a cost to one's self-esteem. In effect, the Comparison Level of Alternatives has a different meaning within a stable relationship. The classical effects appear to be more characteristic of an already deteriorating relationship or a nonrelationship.

Interdependence as a Dynamical Concept

I have made three basic points thus far. First, exchange and development involve changes in levels or types of interdependence. Second, interdependence can be modeled in terms of certain aspects of how complex, dynamical systems form and change. Third, given this way of framing exchange and development, similar principles hold across different types of core configurations (Caporael and Baron, 1997). These basic principles are robust across dyadic, intragroup, and intergroup patterns of change, given the assumption that development is a species of change from simple to more complex levels of functioning.

It is now possible to use microdynamical concepts to facilitate a uniform treatment of exchange and development given that both exchange and development involve changes in interdependence. For example, the shift from exchange to communal orientation has been treated as a shift from two individuals using each other to maximize individual outcomes to a situation where I or Me thinking shifts to a We orientation. Viewed this way, there is a social developmental process linking exchange and communal orientation. That is, within a We orientation, there is a reciprocal or mutual focus on complementary need satisfaction. This shift involves a phase transition from an individual mode of social organization to a collective level of organization. In the communal mode, the other, to use Buber's (1970) morally apt terms, enters into an I-Thou (you) relation instead of an I-It relation. Developmentally, the other must be seen as a you before a sense of "We-ness" can emerge.

Once this occurs, basic exchange concepts such as Comparison Level of Alternatives can be given a collective interpretation. In dynamical systems terms, we move from local to global dynamics. Formally, such change is self-organized, allowing for a collapse of individual degrees of freedom at the collective level while simultaneously increasing degrees of freedom for the collective structure. Where in this formulation does exchange enter? Extending Clark and Mills's (1993) terms, exchange is viewed as a phase state, involving a tit-for-tat regulated type of interdependence, whereas communal interdependence is regulated not by equity but rather by a type of mutual sensitivity to a partner's need. In sum, the modification treats both exchange and communal relations as forms of interdependence in that in both situations, self-other outcomes are yoked; however, the meaning of reciprocity shifts from an I-driven calculation of fair returns to a We-driven feeling that I cannot be happy if the other is in need.

The Relevance of Dynamical Concepts

Given this description, can we make use of specific dynamical concepts such as attractor, control parameter, and order parameter? One possible move, given that we treat exchange and communal as different phase state modalities, is to assume they have different attractor states, where by *attractor*, I refer to goal states at a collective level. One could demonstrate this in a number of ways. One strategy goes back to a demonstration by Horwitz (1954) that people who believed they would interact in the future with the people they were working with to solve problems showed better memory for group-level incomplete tasks than for individually incomplete tasks. The reverse was true for people who did not expect to have future interactions; this difference demonstrates a group Zeigarnik effect. Applying this reasoning to the exchange and communal situation, we would expect an individual Zeigarnik effect for the exchange mode situation and a group Zeigarnik effect for the communal or We level of organization. For example, in an earlier study described by Asch (1952), Zeigarnik effects do not occur if one's partner completes the task.

In this context, what disrupts or perturbs functioning in the exchange situation and the communal situation is likely to be different. For example, increasing group size might improve functioning in a communal setting because need-based compatibility is likely to increase with a larger pool of others. Furthermore, creating a jigsaw situation where people's solutions of problems require a sharing of resources would likely help stabilize a communal situation by articulating complementary roles. Size, however, is likely to interfere with a tit-for-tat type of reasoning because it would likely overload the social accounting process. That is, it is more difficult to evaluate equity with different types of contributions from more people.

A dynamical way of viewing this relation is to assume that exchange and communal attractors are in a periodic, cyclical relation to one another. In such a situation, the output of one phase is the input that triggers the reverse mode. For example, a certain level of equity might function as a control parameter for communal relations to kick in, and a certain deterioration in sensitivity to others' needs could lead a communal relation to shift to an exchange mode where people begin to keep score again. Such effects are likely to be nonlinear; a small decrease in perceived sensitivity to need could lower trust and result in a shift from communal to exchange, given certain initial conditions. Such phase shifts may show hysteresis. The level of trust that allowed a shift from exchange to communal mode will not restore a communal phase once it regresses to exchange-type social regulation; greater trust will be needed.

The order parameters in such a situation would involve demonstrating that a different pattern of part-part or part-whole relations holds for exchange versus communal modes of organization. For example, under an exchange rule, who carries out a given role is not important so long as the role occupant matches his or her efforts with outcomes. In a communal relationship, specific complementary configurations of needs and need-satisfying resources must be coordinated to achieve a stable system.

Refining the Concepts

The basic strategy of the dynamical-complex systems view of exchange and development has been to use interdependence as the vehicle for introducing dynamical concepts to model exchange and development. Now we are ready to make the case in stronger terms, arguing that the dynamical-complex systems approach is necessary if we want to treat exchange and development as more than individual-level constructs and phenomena.

The first step toward making this case involves proposing that development should be viewed as dynamical, self-organized change, where the relations between wholes and parts are repeatedly reassembled. That is, development is, in effect, a description of the changing pattern of part-whole relations over time. This means we need to think about change at the level of a system, where relations among parts are constantly being reorganized. For example, the same people function as individuals, as parts of dyads, and as parts of groups. More pointedly, the same people go from task to socio-emotional phases in a group, participate in majority and minority influence relations, and are involved in exchange and communal relationships. What differs is how part-part and part-whole relations are configured in regard to how the same individual fits into different role systems. According to this view, individual and group are not opposed units of functioning; the individual is in the group, and the group is in the individual.

One way to describe these different configurations is to identify how attractors differ for different collective states where by *attractor,* I refer to a place in the phase state toward which individual trajectories are drawn or converge. For example, when majority influence is the dominant-group phase state, consensus is the attractor toward which all patterns of influence are drawn; cognitively, this is expressed by forces toward convergent thinking and away from divergent forms of information expression. With minority influence dominant, diversity becomes the attractor, with divergent inputs encouraged by group forces. In terms of configurations, with majority influence the system has strong social ties and strong bonding analogous to ice. When minority influence dominates, the strength of ties is weaker and the system is more like water. In the extreme case of loose ties, group forces are dissipated, as in the case of gas.

Which group control parameter is analogous to changes in temperature? Some candidates include group size in general and the size of minority or deviant faction in particular. When people are strangers, even a single ally can break the majority's power. Here, the discrepant situation shifts from a deviant to one of minority influence. Another approach is to invoke something like Latane's social impact theory (1981) to predict phase transitions; that is, while just one ally can have substantial impact, each additional ally may be expected to have less effect given an extrapolation from the influence of size on majority influence. However, with minority influence, consistency may be an important control parameter, so that even a single deviant, if consistent over trials, may sway a majority (Moscovici and Nemeth, 1974). At issue here may be over how many trials and how early was the dissent. In such a situation, consistent deviant input may weaken the strength of the ties between majority members over time. For example, when individual doubt levels reach a certain threshold, social ties may be weakened between majority members. Indeed, groupthink (Janis, 1982) may be viewed as a kind of anticipatory strategy that prevents the use of minority influence.

We may extrapolate further from research and theory on the relation between the size of predator and prey populations (Baron, Amazeen, and Beek, 1994). Specifically, the size of each population coregulates the other's so that neither the prey nor the predator population gains control or predominates. The correct ratio is critical, given the resources available in a given niche. Similarly, looking at a group over time, the most effective problem solving is likely to occur when a certain balance holds between the strength of the minority and the strength of the majority. A similar argument can be made for the relative amount of time that a group is dominated by task and socioemotional concerns.

I propose that the stability of a social relationship may follow similar principles. Thus, contrary to existing theory, a relationship should be most stable if there is a regular cycling between exchange and communal types of attractors. That is, it is proposed that an exchange orientation with its social accounting to establish equity is too demanding of cognitive resources, whereas a communal relationship where need predominates over equity is likely to become one-sided eventually to the extent one or the other person feels cheated or exploited at some level (Pratto and Walker, 2000). Moreover, for the more needy person, accepting help without reciprocating may eventually result in lower self-esteem (Aron, Aron, Tudor, and Nelson, 1991). Thus, at a collective level, what is called for is a periodic attractor regime—a situation that is intermediate in complexity between the stability and simplicity of a single homeostatic point attractor like consensus and yet less complex than a chaotic regime, where even the smallest difference in initial conditions makes for massive changes in the trajectory and functioning of the system. In effect, we want to steer a course between the sterile stability of groupthink and the extreme openness of constant social splintering.

In the examples already provided, interdependence is given a highly dynamic interpretation at a collective level. Furthermore, development is viewed as nonlinear and complex. Specifically, development is not directed toward a set end state; rather, it involves steering a course between order and disorder. This type of complexity in rapidly changing environments is likely to be most adaptive at the edge of chaos, because it is in this state that change is most likely to be self-generated in relation to the positive feedback mechanisms of self-organized criticality. Viewed in this way, development is a never-finished process of shifting attractors and circular causality where we create structures that then shape us.

This model offers a variety of interpretations of exchange. First, like development, exchange is a form of interdependence. However, development is treated largely as a process of change, whereas exchange is a description of a phase state, analogous to distinguishing between ice and water. As such, it is related to other phase states with different attractors. For example, equity is the attractor for exchange relationships, whereas "from each according to need" is the attractor for communal relationships. Furthermore, the dynamical model gives us a way of specifying how interdependence between attractors might develop and maintain itself. Indeed, one could describe many aspects of social development in terms of how qualitatively different attractors are brought into a dynamical system relationship.

A particularly good example of development in a social relations sense is Kelman's (1997) use of conflict resolution workshops between Palestinians and Israelis to produce "uneasy coalitions," a concept that might also be brought to bear in the relation between exchange and communal attractors. Whatever the current state of Arab-Israeli relations, Kelman has helped to create a situation where interdependence can no longer be readily denied. Such interdependence has two major foci. First, achieving positive self- and group identity for each group need not constitute a zero-sum identity game, where for one group to feel good, the other has to lose face. Second, once identity is not threatened, uneasy coalitions between conflicting groups are created. A broader way to frame this dynamic relation is to assume that for peace negotiations to maintain credibility with their originating groups, personal bonds between negotiators cannot be too strong. That is, what is at issue is coordinating two qualitatively different attractors: intragroup solidarity and intergroup cooperation.

One way to frame this problem, which is also relevant for framing the dynamical relation between communal and exchange attractors, is to assume that intergroup cooperation and in-group solidarity function as periodic attractors that cycle in and out of salience depending on certain moderating conditions, including the strength and duration of the alternating attractor phase states. When intergroup cooperation gets too strong, the alternative attractor of in-group solidarity is triggered. In such a system, the output of one phase becomes the input that triggers the opposed phase state.

Implications of the Dynamical Model

Given this phasic view of interdependence, what are the implications for a dynamical view of exchange and development? First, let us use as a model the work of Gersick (1989), who suggests that one possible control parameter for how task and socioemotional factors develop an interphase is close-ness to a temporal deadline. Specifically, across a wide range of tasks and time intervals, Gersick (1989) finds that "a major transition in groups' approach toward their work occurs at the midpoint of their allotted work" (p. 271). In terms of this analysis, it could be argued that at the midpoint, task and socioemotional factors become organized in a maximally effective ratio, thereby freeing up the problem-solving process for creative thinking.

This midpoint principle might then be extrapolated to individual social development; the growth of social linkages of increasing interdependence probably plateaus at middle age and then decreases. As we approach the midpoint of our lives, a certain ordering may occur in regard to the relative salience of exchange and communal attractors. At a more molecular level, we take such development to be predicated on the ability to enter into and respect joint commitments, which some consider the hallmark of sociality (Baron, Amazeen, and Beek, 1994; Gilbert, 1996). Specifically, once joint commitments are in place, such social arrangements cannot be breached unilaterally without violating one's responsibilities to the relationship. To do so would be a form of social cheating, a form that cannot be satisfied by a simple equity rule. Thus, exchange- and communal-level social cheating may be different. For example, in a one-sided divorce, a situation where one partner unilaterally walks out, the hurt will not be assuaged by an equal division of property or perhaps not even by a very generous division of property. Specifically, a marriage is a special exemplar of a class of situations where a partner cannot legitimately leave without permission of the other.

Developmentally, we need social skills to enter into and maintain joint commitments, and we need to value the jointness of this relationship so that actions take the form of a "we" orientation. This means that relationships cannot be legitimately dissolved or repaired unilaterally. What has been added is a moral dimension that weighs both what is done and how it is done. Thus, leaving a marriage may be morally correct if it is joint, but not if it is done unilaterally, and particularly if done without notice. Morality in this sense is inextricably bound to sociality.

Thus, once people enter into close relationships, communal rules supersede individual exchange justifications. It may then be assumed that these rules stabilize relationships, thereby conveying evolutionary benefit by protecting the offspring of the union. It is in this context, for example, that walking out on a marriage with young children may be considered "more wrong" than leaving a partner in a childless marriage. There is a com-monality between Kelman's (1997) peace negotiation work and this mar-riage example; both types of relationships are uneasy coalitions. Whatever the level of the joint commitment—dyadic, between members and the group, or between two groups—there is always a part-whole tension. Specifically, attempts to maximize individual goals lead one to join groups and, at the same time, create a potential conflict between individual and new group goals. However, both exchange and communal principles may work in concert. We enter into social relationships because they offer superior outcomes to what we can achieve as individuals.

We stay in relationships, however, for two sets of reasons: one rooted in exchange and the other in communal principles. At an exchange level, we stay as long as there are favorable Comparison Level of Alternatives. This, however, provides an unstable basis for collectivity. A stronger basis for staying in groups is that joint commitment creates forces that entrain individual goals to the collectivity even when Comparison Level of Alternative considerations would dissolve the social relationship. We learn or are evolutionarily prepared that it is wrong to break a joint agreement unilaterally. In Buber's (1970) moralistic terms, to do so would involve treating the other as an It rather than as a You, who has now become the occasion for "We-ness." Thus, in the ideal social relationship, we stay with others both to maximize outcomes and to do the right thing.

At a molar level, this type of I-You frame self-organizes dyadic framings of this problem into the formation of a group in which jointness of commitment is expressed in terms of norms regarding the responsibilities of members to groups and of groups to members. Furthermore, this dynamical relation at the group level may be seen as taking the form of majority versus minority relations as opposed to individual versus group relations. This, in turn, may be framed at the collective level in terms of the relative prepotency of attractors favoring convergent and divergent thinking. This situation also has a moral edge to it; we readily condemn groupthink that lacks a significant divergent-minority faction. This is typically seen as bad, perhaps because it violates an implicit constraint of jointness, where here reciprocity is expressed in terms of majority and minority factions respecting each other's domains of influence. This respect may be expressed dynamically, in terms of a periodic coordination of convergent and divergent attractors. For example, a cycling of such attractors may occur as a form of coordination at a molar level, with certain periods of group activity dominated by minority influence and other periods by majority-type thinking, norms, and values. Development involves changes in the proportion of time allocated to minority and majority agendas.

Indeed, at a collective level, this cycling may give us an uneasy coalition between phase states that describes both the readiness of this group for change and the readiness of this group to engage in intergroup cooperation on certain dimensions. Such an analysis provides a dynamical view of group development by reframing interdependence in terms of coordinations between collective states rather than individuals.

The basic units that change when phase state organizations occur are people in group-constrained roles. For example, if a group is part of an organization, it is hypothesized that a shift from task to socioemotional functioning involves a shift from a vertical to horizontal orderings.

Conclusion

Social development at the individual level involves an increasing capacity to become communal, as, for example, when dyadic social relationships move from an equity exchange attractor mode to a communal need-based mode. However, this too is phasic; development is nearer to a circle than a straight line. To elaborate, the existing approach to development differs from other stage theories of development. Thus, there is clearly a progression in level of achievement along certain dimensions; whether cognitive reasoning, moral development, or social competence, there are certain core problems that persist within and across levels. I propose that the I to We shift—in broader terms, the exchange to communal orientation shift—is a core problem that appears early (once the child can differentiate self from other) and repeatedly reasserts itself throughout the life cycle. Why? Because achieving interdependence successfully, albeit in the context of different life tasks and different constraints, is a persisting problem across adolescence, emerging adulthood, and middle or old age.

From this frame, I propose that exchange and communal modes constitute as basic a dimension of development as autonomy and relatedness. And just as it can be argued that autonomy and relatedness are complementary rather than opposed dimensions (Arnett, 2000), so too can exchange and communal modes be treated as complementary. Thus, given the existing view of the relation between exchange and development, I literally mean that the more things change, the more they remain the same.

References

Arnett, J. J. "Emerging Adulthood: A Theory of Development from the Late Teens Through the Twenties." *American Psychologist,* 2000, *55,* 469–480.

Aron, A., Aron, E. N., Tudor, M., and Nelson, G. "Close Relationships as Including the Other in the Self." *Journal of Personality and Social Psychology,* 1991, *60,* 241–253.

Aronson, E., Stephen, C., Sikes, J., Blaney, N., and Shapp, M. *The Jigsaw Classroom.* Thousand Oaks, Calif.: Sage, 1978.

Arrow, H., McGrath J. E., and Bardahl, J. L. *Small Groups as Complex Systems: Formation, Coordination, Development, and Adaptation.* Thousand Oaks, Calif.: Sage, 2000.

Asch, S. E. *Social Psychology.* Upper Saddle River, N.J.: Prentice Hall, 1952.

Bak, P. *How Nature Works: The Science of Self-Organized Criticality.* New York: Copernicus Books, 1996.

Bales, R. F. "Task-Roles and Social Roles in Problem-Solving Groups." In E. E. Maccoby, T. M. Newcomb, and E. L. Hartley (eds.), *Readings in Social Psychology.* (3rd ed.) New York: Henry Holt, 1958.

Baron, R. M., Amazeen, P. G., and Beek P. J. "Local and Global Dynamics of Social Relations." In R. R. Vallacher and A. Nowak (eds.), *Dynamical Systems in Social Psychology.* Orlando, Fla.: Academic Press, 1994.

Buber, M. *I and Thou.* New York: Scribner, 1970.

Buss, L. W. *The Evolution of Individuality.* Princeton, N.J.: Princeton University Press, 1987.

Campbell, D. T. "Common Fate Similarity and Other Indices of Status Aggregates of Persons as Social Entities." *Behavioral Science,* 1958, 2, 14–25.

Campbell, D. T. "Levels of Organization, Downward Causation, and the Selection-Theory Approach to Evolutionary Epistemology." In G. Greenberg and E. Tobach (eds.), *Theories of the Evolution of Knowing.* Mahwah, N.J.: Erlbaum, 1990.

Caporael, L. R., and Baron, R. M. "Groups as the Mind's Natural Environment." In J. A. Simpson and D. T. Kenrick (eds.), *Evolutionary Social Psychology.* Mahwah, N.J.: Erlbaum, 1997.

Clark, M. S., and Mills, J. "The Difference Between Communal and Exchange Relationships: What It Is and Is Not." *Personality and Social Psychology Bulletin,* 1993, 19, 684–691.

Gersick, C.J.C. "Marking Time: Predictable Transitions in Task Groups." *Academy of Management Journal,* 1989, 32, 274–309.

Gilbert, M. *Living Together: Rationality, Sociality, and Obligation.* Lanham, Md.: Rowman & Littlefield, 1996.

Granovetter, M. S. "The Strength of Weak Ties." *American Journal of Sociology,* 1973, 78, 1360–1380.

Green, J. A., and Gustafson, G. E., "Perspectives on an Ecological Approach to Social Communicative Development in Infancy." In C. Dent-Read and P. Zukow-Goldring (eds.), *Evolving Explanations of Development.* Washington, D.C.: American Psychological Association, 1997.

Harris, J. R. "Where Is the Child's Environment? A Group Socialization Theory of Development." *Psychological Review,* 1995, 102, 458–489.

Hatfield, E. "Passionate and Companionate Love." In R. Sternberg and M. L. Barnes (eds.), *The Psychology of Love.* New Haven, Conn.: Yale University Press, 1988.

Horwitz, M. "The Recall of Interrupted Group Tasks: An Experimental Study of Individual Motivation in Relation to Group Goals." *Human Relations,* 1954, 7, 3–38.

Janis, I. L. *Groupthink.* (2nd ed.) Boston: Houghton Mifflin, 1982.

Kelman, H. "Group Processes in Resolution of International Conflict: Experiences from the Israeli-Palestinian Case." *American Psychologist,* 1997, 52, 212–220.

Kelso, J.A.S. *Dynamic Patterns: The Self-Organization of Brain and Behavior Complex Adaptive Systems.* Cambridge, Mass.: Bradford Books, 1995.

Latane, B. "The Psychology of Social Impact." *American Psychologist,* 1981, 36, 343–356.

Levine, J. M., and Moreland, R. "Small Groups." In D. Gilbert, S. Fiske, and G. Lindzey (eds.), *Handbook of Social Psychology.* New York: McGraw-Hill, 1998.

Levinger, G. "Toward the Analysis of Close Relationships." *Journal of Experimental Social Psychology,* 1980, 16, 510–544.

Lewin, K. "Group Decision and Social Change." In T. Newcomb and E. Hartley (eds.), *Readings in Social Psychology.* New York: Henry Holt, 1947.

Moreland, R. L., and Levine, J. M. "Socialization in Small Groups: Temporal Changes in Individual-Group Relations." In L. Berkowitz (ed.), *Advances in Experimental Social Psychology.* Vol. 15. Orlando, Fla.: Academic Press, 1982.

Moscovici, S., and Nemeth, C. "Minority Influence." In C. Nemeth (ed.), *Social Psychology: Classic and Contemporary Integrations."* Skokie, Ill.: Rand McNally, 1974.

Nowak, A., and Vallacher, R. R. *Dynamical Social Psychology.* New York: Guilford Press, 1998.

Pratto, F., and Walker, A. "Dominance in Disguise: Power, Beneficence, and Exploitation in Personal Relationships." In A. Lee-Chai and J. A. Bargh (eds.), *The Use and Abuse of Power: Multiple Perspectives on the Causes of Corruption.* Philadelphia: Psychology Press, 2000.

Prigogine, I., and Stengers, I. *Order Out of Chaos: Man's New Dialogue with Nature.* New York: Bantam Books, 1984.

Rusbult, C. "Response to Dissatisfaction in Close Relationships: The Exit-Voice-Loyalty-Neglect Model." In D. Perlman and S. Duck (eds.), *Development, Dynamics, and Deterioration.* Thousand Oaks, Calif.: Sage, 1987.

Sternberg, R. J. "Liking Versus Loving: A Comparative Evaluation of Theories." *Psychological Bulletin,* 1987, *102,* 331–345.

Thelen, E. "Learning to Walk: Ecological Demands and Phylogenetic Constraints." In L. P. Lipsett and C. Rovee-Collier (eds.), *Advances in Infancy Research.* Vol. 3. Norwood, N.J.: Ablex, 1984.

Thibaut, J. W., and Kelley, H. H. *The Social Psychology of Groups.* New York: Wiley, 1959.

Turvey, M. T. "Coordination." *American Psychologist,* 1990, *45,* 938–953.

Van Geert, P. "The Dynamics of General Developmental Mechanisms: From Piaget and Vygotsky to Dynamic Systems Models." *Current Directions in Psychological Science,* 2000, *9,* 64–88.

Vygotsky, L. S. *Mind in Society: The Development of Higher Psychological Processes* (M. Cole and others, eds.). Cambridge, Mass.: Harvard University Press, 1978.

REUBEN M. BARON is emeritus professor of psychology at the University of Connecticut.

5

Guided by evolutionary theory, the authors propose that factors such as developmental context and genetic relatedness may fundamentally alter social exchange processes.

Evolutionary Perspectives on the Development of Social Exchanges

Brad E. Sheese, William G. Graziano

In recent years, the study of relationships and the study of development have become more integrated (Collins and Laursen, 1999). Researchers have begun to explore beyond infancy in order to understand how development through childhood and adolescence affects relationships and how relationships affect development. Social exchange has played a minimal role in this integration, in part because social exchange and developmental perspectives appear incompatible in a number of ways (Maccoby, 1999). We argue that these incompatibilities can be resolved by using evolutionary theories to extend the logic of social exchange, discuss the implications of an expanded evolutionary perspective on social exchange and development, and tentatively explore an even broader perspective based on multilevel selection theories.

Definitions are important to this chapter because some controversial issues hinge on how different theorists use the same terms. First, we assume that social exchange represents a basic set or family of interpersonal processes that appear in all cultures, which make coordinated social behavior possible. They are emergent from social interaction and are not primarily a characteristic of individual persons. Furthermore, we assume that all cultures have a major stake in enculturating children with rules of social exchange, socializing them to know what it means to follow the rules and what it means to be a cheater. We define social exchange as processes that involve interactions between at least two persons in which control of commodities transfers from one person to the other. In this chapter, we do not assume that the persons in the exchange are social equals, that the commodities being exchanged are necessarily tangible, or that the exchange is free of constraint. We assume that social exchange is a basic behavioral phenomenon that can appear in different forms in persons of different developmental levels. The different forms may or may not have similar functions.

Second, in this chapter *development* refers to a relatively enduring transformation of central psychological structures. We assume that many, but not all, of the transformations are irreversible. We assume that development is not the same as learning, although some forms of learning may also be irreversible. Social development, then, refers to an output: relatively enduring changes in social behavior, social cognition, and socially relevant affect that occur as a result of transformations in central psychological structures.

We can now move from basic definitions to a consideration of social exchange theories, which appear to make certain assumptions that may be useful for understanding adult social behavior but are less useful for understanding social development. Often, the assumptions are not stated explicitly, and we admit freely that the list encompasses inferences that are arguable. First, social exchange theories seem to assume that the substantive nature of the relationship makes little difference to the exchange process. Put another way, social exchange processes occur across cultures, in business relations, in kin interaction, and in romantic relations, but the process is basically the same across relationship classes. To be sure, theoretical work has suggested some exceptions to this assumption. Some notable exceptions are Kelley and Thibaut's discussion (1978) of the transformation of the given matrix into the effective matrix, the Clark and Mills (1979) distinction between communal and exchange relationships, and the recent theoretical work by Costanzo (1991) on mother-child interactions. Nevertheless, the overall thrust of social exchange theories is to suggest that underlying relationship processes are similar across kinds of relationships. The working assumption seems to be that different kinds of relationships differ in mean level of this or that parameter, not in underlying processes (in contrast, see Graziano, 1987; Jensen-Campbell and Graziano, 2000).

One consequence of this assumption is to narrow empirical activity to one kind of relationship, preferably one that is convenient to study. Much like the learning researchers who conducted research on white laboratory rats, social exchange theorists have directed their attention to relationships among young adults who are relative equals and operate within a relatively open field. The empirical literature on social exchange processes is not hospitable to persons interested in transformation of persons because the working assumption seems to be that there are no meaningful transformations (in contrast, see Foa and Foa, 1980). Are mother-child exchanges really based on the same underlying process as social exchanges among young adult peers? Are exchanges among non-age-mates based on the same underlying processes as those among age-mates (for instance, Graziano, 1978)?

In the absence of alternative empirical evidence or theoretical arguments to the contrary, it was reasonable to assume that all relationships are similar. However, just as learning researchers came to recognize that biological differences between species produced different constraints on learning processes, relationship researchers have become increasingly cognizant of potential differences in processes across relationship types or domains (see Bugental, 2000, for an overview). For example, theory from evolutionary social psychology suggests that relationships differ in important ways from each other, and evolution has shaped separate, distinct modules or algorithms of the mind to deal with them in different ways (Bugental, 2000; Buss, 2000; Tooby and Cosmides, 1992). These modules may be differentially sensitive to different aspects of the environment. The mother-child relationship, for example, seems to have special status as a relationship due to its close association with infant survival (for instance, Bartholomew and Shaver, 1998; Bowlby, 1969). The processes underlying mother-infant relationships, and the associated social exchange processes, may be one manifestation of an evolution-prepared mind. Mother-infant exchanges appear in a sophisticated form very early in development, and they may depend on an underlying process that has little or no continuity with later social relationships (for instance, Lewis, 2001; Lewis, Feiring, and Rosenthal, 2000). We may assume continuity, and we may posit consistency across relationship types by talking of internal working models, but these are assumptions that should be explored empirically. When continuity is explicitly examined, surprisingly little is found (Lewis, Feiring, and Rosenthal, 2000).

If this line of thinking is correct, then it may imply that the transformations that define social development are not unitary. Social development may be a fragmented process, in which some modules and kinds of social exchanges produce sophisticated output well before other modules. More important, it is possible that the underlying processes of social exchanges across classes or domains of relationships may be different and show different developmental trajectories. Either way, from a practical standpoint, it is unlikely we will ever discover differences if we do not test and explore the assumption that all relationships flow from the same fundamental underlying process.

Basic Themes

The assumptions of social exchange theory have implications for the study of social development. However, before we discuss these implications, it is necessary to lay out the framework of a basic social exchange model. To do this, we begin with a classic yet simple question: Why do human adults engage in social relations at all? In theory, individuals engage in relationships to receive benefits that cannot be attained without some form of assistance. From this perspective, we are social primarily because it is beneficial for us to be social. More simply, we are social because it serves our individual purposes. This sort of self-centered and essentially hedonistic approach to social relations has a long history in psychology, philosophy, and, of course, economics. However, social exchange theory also suggests that by giving our partners what they need and receiving from our partners what we need (engaging in exchanges), over time we develop expectations about future exchanges, and ultimately we become interdependent. At some point, the relationship itself becomes valuable. In this respect, social exchange theory departs from traditional economic models in that it suggests that relationships themselves, and not just exchanges, are of consequence.

Social exchange theory also addresses the dissolution of relationships through the use of comparison levels (Walster, Walster, and Berscheid, 1978; Kelley and Thibaut, 1978). The comparison-level concept suggests that we show consistency across relationships as a result of the development of expectations about what we should be receiving in our social exchanges. This expectation resembles an evolutionary historicity effect in that evolution may have prepared a module for a particular kind of relationship, but the individual's actual life experience creates a working document (Graziano and Tobin, 1999). This looks remarkably like a transformed central psychological structure. Thibaut and Kelley (1959) expanded the comparison-level concept further in their notion of Comparison Level for Alternatives. Whereas the comparison level reflects an individual's life history, the Comparison Level for Alternatives adds interpersonal elements to the social exchange through social comparison. If a person's current relationship has a better cost-to-benefit ratio than alternatives, then the person is relatively satisfied and will stay in the relationship. If we stretch the concept a bit, the two comparison-level ideas allow us to answer our "Why be social?" question in a slightly more formal way. If the relative ratio of costs and benefits for engaging in a relationship exceeds the relative costs and benefits of not being in a relationship, then it makes sense to engage in a relationship. The comparison-level idea also speaks to targets: With whom should any given person have a relationship? Different individuals offer different cost-benefit ratios as relationship partners, so we select the best cost-benefit ratio available.

This social exchange framework revolving around needs, expectations, future interactions, and comparisons of benefits can be applied to most relationships. Of course, the currency of exchange will vary both between and within relationships, but the ultimate answer as to why we engage in any given relationship and why we pick particular people over others to engage in relationships does not change. We have relationships with people because it benefits us to do so, and we prefer people who provide a lot of benefit without a lot of cost. The entire logic of social exchange can also be extended to explain an individual's participation in a group. Presumably, the group provides something to the individuals in the group that the individuals are unable to attain by themselves. In return for this benefit, the individuals provide some form of contribution to the group. If all goes well, interdependence between an individual and the group will develop over time as exchanges continue and expectations are established. Finally, satisfaction with group membership should depend on the relative costs and benefits of belonging to one group in comparison with belonging to some alternative group or being by oneself.

On its face, this sort of cost-benefit analysis implies that people ruthlessly exploit each other for personal gain in an endless orgy of opportunism. However, research suggests that when it comes to relationships, most people more closely resemble bargain hunters rather than shoplifters. People seem to want a good deal in relationships, not an outright steal (Gergen, 1974; Gergen, Ellsworth, Maslach, and Seipel, 1975; Walster, Walster, and Berscheid, 1978). Exploiting people may lead to short-term benefits, but in most social ecologies, there are long-term costs for such behavior. Ultimately, selfish concerns are opposed by dependence on future interactions with others for continued success. These concerns for equity are still self-serving, but certainly they are preferable to the alternative.

As a whole, the social exchange model offers a useful and relatively comprehensive framework for studying the development, maintenance, and dissolution of adult dyadic relationships, and perhaps even group relationships. However, we propose that social exchange models are incomplete. To understand why, it is helpful to consider some developmental aspects of social relationships.

Learning to Love Your Mother?

Social exchange models describe a process wherein individuals maximize their benefits and rewards by engaging in interactions with others. From a socialization perspective, the only prerequisites to engaging in this process would appear to be a healthy dose of self-interest and an ability to learn. Fortunately, children have both. Young children come supplied with a great number of needs, and consequently self-interest, but little else. To meet these needs, children are dependent on their caregivers; however, care is not provided unconditionally. Children learn that in order to have their needs met, they must conform to their caregiver's expectations. This account describes the general process of socialization through which children acquire values, attitudes, expectations, and presumably the rules of engaging in social relationships (Bugental and Goodnow, 1998; Costanzo, 1991; Jones and Gerard, 1967).

Direct learning provides a simple account of the acquisition (but not the development) of a social exchange orientation. However, both direct learning and the social exchange model seem ill equipped to account for mother-infant relationships (Maccoby, 1999). First, social exchange models propose that relationships develop over time through a series of interactions. This suggests that interdependence in relationships develops in a relatively gradual manner. It would be difficult, however, to describe a mother's initial response to her child as indifference or even cautious optimism. Initial encounters between infant and mother bear little resemblance to most initial encounters between business associates or even romantic partners. Instead, there appear to be a variety of mechanisms to ensure a nearly unconditional bond between mothers and their infants. Both mothers and infants come "prepared" for the relationship. That is not to say that this bond cannot be degraded through unresponsive parenting or enhanced through responsive parenting. On the contrary, sensitive parenting is clearly important. However, neither the infant nor the mother would appear to spend a lot of time assessing whether the other is a worthy, reciprocating relationship partner.

Second, children are poorly equipped to meet their own needs and are consequently dependent on others to do so. This is particularly true in infancy. Most mother-infant relationships are clearly characterized by interdependence. Mothers and infants are mutually solicitous and responsive. However, on the whole, the relative costs and benefits to the mother and the infant appear dramatically skewed (Maccoby, 1999). In part, this is because we are an altricial species. When infants are born, they are entirely unable to care for themselves. They pose a huge drain on both the physical and psychological resources of their parents. It is clear why an infant would maintain a relationship with its mother; the benefit to the infant is its continued survival. What is not clear is what exactly constitutes the huge benefit to the mother that makes up for all of the costs. It is very difficult (although not impossible) to answer this question in terms of a rational cost-benefit analysis (Maccoby, 1999; also see Walster, Walster, and Berscheid, 1978). In fact, children are a resource drain long after infancy. This inequity is most pronounced in early infancy, but it is a persistent problem in any family relationship.

One solution to these problems is to suggest that the mother-infant relationship, and indeed any other relationship that does not exhibit overt characteristics of an exchange relationship, is, in fact, not an exchange relationship. It could be argued that this relationship is an altogether different kind of relationship that does not revolve around the selfishness that drives exchange relationships. For example, Clark (1984; Clark and Mills, 1979; Chapter One, this volume) refers to a relationship in which the partners show a concern for, and respond to, each other's needs without an expectation of an immediate and equivalent return as a communal relationship. Another alternative, provided by Fiske (1991, 1992), proposes that there are four different kinds of basic social relations, only one of which matches an exchange relationship as we have described it.

In contrast, we propose that relationships such as the mother-infant relationship can still be understood in terms of the general social exchange framework. However, to do so, we must consider costs and benefits at a different level of analysis.

Neo-Darwinian Evolutionary Approaches to Social Behavior

Evolutionary psychology (Buss, 1995, 2000) is also concerned with costs and benefits to individuals as they relate to social behavior and relationships. However, because reproduction represents a kind of ultimate goal, costs and benefits in evolutionary terms usually refer to things that either improve or impede reproductive fitness. For a long while, evolutionary thinkers were concerned with why we would ever do anything for others (increase their reproductive fitness at a cost to our own) if our only goal were to maximize our own fitness. This question bears more than a passing resemblance to our original question about why people bother to engage in relationships.

The answer provided by the neo-Darwinian theories developed in the 1970s and 1980s also parallels social exchange theories. Trivers (1971) proposed that cooperative behavior among nonrelated individuals could be explained by reciprocal altruism, which suggests that helping others can be advantageous (increase fitness) as long as the beneficiary helps the benefactor in return. However, there is always a danger that people will receive benefits but not return benefits. So how do people avoid exploitation? The answer is that people do unto others as they have been done unto. Using computer simulations, Axelrod and Hamilton (1981) showed that a tit-for-tat strategy, wherein an agent initially cooperated and subsequently did whatever the partner had done on the previous turn, proved to be a viable strategy. Repeated interactions are the key (see Nowak and Sigmund, 1998, for a different perspective). If two persons, A and B, interact once and never see each other again, there is no simple way for A to ensure he or she will not be exploited by B or vice versa. But if A is to interact with B repeatedly (that is, to form some kind of relationship), as long as there are mechanisms to remember and punish exploiters, it is in everyone's best interest to cooperate. Furthermore, Roberts and Sherratt (1998) proposed that a strategy of escalating altruism is viable. Their raise-the-stakes strategy starts with small, positive exchanges; if these exchanges are reciprocated, the investment increases. In essence, their strategy succeeds by slowly building trust. The parallels between reciprocal altruism and the social exchange model are striking. Relationships are established, maintained, and dissolved for the same reasons and through the same processes. The primary difference is that evolutionary theories specifically describe costs and benefits in terms of fitness.

In addition, in contrast to social exchange theory, evolutionary theory can easily account for mother-infant relationships. The concept of inclusive fitness (Hamilton, 1964a, 1964b) provides a general framework for describing relations with all of our kin. Inclusive fitness shifts the cost-benefit analysis yet again; costs and benefits are defined not in terms of the reproductive fitness of the individual but rather in terms of the reproductive fitness of the genes. Put simply, if we assume that our ultimate goal is not the reproduction of ourselves but rather the reproduction of our genes, and that we share our genes with our kin, then helping kin in some circumstances will increase the fitness of our genes. Inclusive fitness suggests that if we are related to the person we are helping, then we are, in a way, helping ourselves (or at least our genes). Therefore, in terms of social exchange, simply being related to the other person in the relationship provides some degree of benefit that offsets potential costs. Furthermore, the more related you are, the more indirect benefit you receive when you help your kin. In the case of a mother and newborn infant, the infant represents a substantial investment with a potentially large payoff for the mother and her genes. Consequently, the infant, should she or he prove to be unable initially to reciprocate and to be a generally poor provider of benefits, is unlikely to be cast aside for someone with a better cost-benefit ratio.

This is not to say people would do anything for their kin. Haldane (1955) suggested that he would risk his life to save two but not one of his brothers. In fact, since you are not 100 percent related to anyone (unless you are an identical twin), including your parents and siblings, your genetic interests and their genetic interests may come into conflict on some occasions. Parent-offspring conflict is a theory that describes such a circumstance (Trivers, 1974). In the classic example of weaning, it is in the best interest of the mother to stop the child from suckling so she can devote resources to another child, but it is in the best interest of the child to continue suckling. Consequently, parent and child come into conflict over when to stop suckling. The mother prefers sooner, the child later. This same genetic cost-benefit logic can be applied to any relationship with kin.

The logic of parent-offspring conflicts illustrates how even the most loving relationships can be framed within a genetic cost-benefit analysis. Consequently, the evolutionary perspective allows us to explain the apparently paradoxical self-sacrificing behavior that characterizes many close relationships and fits so poorly within traditional social exchange models. However, an evolutionary perspective suggests that distinctions may be drawn among different social relationships. At a minimum, there appears to be reason to distinguish among relationship partners along a continuum of genetic relatedness. In addition, Daly, Salmon, and Wilson (1997) suggest that due in part to differential investment strategies, sex of parent also represents a major axis for making distinctions among relationships.

We propose that developmental context represents another such axis. For example, while maximizing fitness could be considered to be a kind of ultimate principle that is consistent across the life span, the goals or tasks associated with maximizing fitness may vary across developmental contexts. For example, a primary goal in infancy may be to elicit caregiving, whereas a primary goal for the postpubescent adolescent is mate seeking. As an individual's goals shift across developmental contexts, benefits and costs are redefined. Consequently, relationships dynamics will also be dependent on shifts in developmental context.

We have suggested that a broad range of relationships, from business relationships to mother-infant relationships, could be better understood by placing social exchange models within a neo-Darwinian evolutionary framework. However, evolutionary theory speaks more to distal than proximal mechanisms. For researchers interested in social development, the adoption of an extended evolutionary framework raises a variety of questions: How do proximal mechanisms develop to support the distal processes described in evolutionary theories? How specialized are the proximal mechanisms? If there are distinct mental modules for, say, kin recognition and cheater detection, how and when do such modules begin functioning? How do these mechanisms function across developmental contexts? For example, one proximal mechanism that may underlie a variety of relationships is empathy, which has been implicated as an important component in the development of children's social relationships (Eisenberg, 2000). However, the bulk of this research has focused on peer relations. Consequently, it is unclear if empathy is equally important in the development of kin and nonkin relationships. Similarly, it is unclear if empathy is differentially important to relationships across developmental contexts. Is empathy more important for getting along with peers than for getting along with siblings? Is empathy more important for parenting early adolescents than young adults? It is possible, even plausible, that empathy is equally important across all combinations of relatedness, sex, and developmental context. However, an evolutionary perspective suggests that generalizabilty should be tested instead of assumed.

Group Selection

A relatively recent, and still controversial, addition to evolutionary approaches is a group selection level of analysis. Group selection refers to the idea, originally proposed by Darwin (1871), that natural selection can sometimes operate on groups as well as on individuals. When group selection occurs, traits can be selected that increase the fitness of the group, not the fitness of the individual or the fitness of the gene. Consequently, it is possible that some forms of social exchange, and the corresponding development of social exchange processes in children, may have produced advantages emerging at the level of groups. Group selection was largely rejected and replaced in the 1960s and 1970s by individual and gene-level theories. Recently, however, Sober and Wilson (1998; Wilson and Sober, 1994) argued that group selection was prematurely and inappropriately dismissed; they posit that group selection does occur and that it might potentially have a large impact on human social evolution.

As we have discussed, both social exchange theories and neo-Darwinian theories offer an essentially self-centered view of human nature: we do things for either ourselves or our genes. Things we do for others are sensible in this context only if they also somehow benefit ourselves or benefit our genes. A group selection level of analysis offers a radically different alternative. Suddenly, it is possible that we can behave in ways that are not beneficial for either us or our genes. Our behavior may make evolutionary sense not because it benefits us but because it benefits the group. Consequently, group selection allows us to consider costs and benefits not from the perspective of the individual or the gene but rather from the perspective of the group.

A multilevel selection perspective encompasses selection at the level of the gene, the level of the individual, and the level of the group (Caporael and Baron, 1997; Wilson, 1997). The integration of a multilevel selection perspective into a social exchange framework would, at a minimum, vastly expand the number of ways in which the costs and benefits of relationships and relationship behaviors can be conceptualized. It would also suggest that what may represent a cost at one level of analysis may simultaneously represent a benefit at another level of analysis. In addition, from this perspective, rather than describing discreet classes of relationships or exchanges, relationship types or relationship domains may be said to describe particular frequently recurrent configurations of costs and benefits across multiple levels of selection.

The application of a multilevel selection perspective to a social exchange framework produces a tremendously, and possibly overwhelmingly, complex perspective on relationships. However, this integrated perspective does suggest some simple, relatively concrete directions that may prove practical to relationship researchers. For example, in classical versions of social exchange theory, a partner's status as a member of an in-group or out-group is of no special importance. In effect, most of the social exchange literature has been restricted to exchanges among members of an in-group. Yet we know from the anthropological literature that significant exchanges do occur between members of different groups. When an in-group member is involved in interactions with out-group members, the exchanges are fraught with complications and constrained by pressure from both sets of in-group members. Capulets should not be forming relationships with Montagues. The group status of interaction partners does matter. In part, in-group members may be concerned that exchanges with out-group members might induce defection, giving away of in-group members' special resources without adequate compensation, or even distortions of in-group power structures as a result of new resources for certain in-group members. Overall, the effects of individual members' social exchanges can have implications for the overall group.

More generally, a multilevel selection perspective suggests that rather than focusing exclusively on individual persons or pairs of persons as the basic units for social exchange processes, the focus could include groups for which social exchange activities have implications. For example, it is possible that children may acquire the rules and norms for social exchanges more readily in group settings than in other settings. This idea is consistent with Piaget's notions about the purpose of games in children's moral development and Vygotsky's notions about the purposes of children's groups. However, the mechanism we propose is different from the ones that Piaget or Vygotsky described. Rather than treating other group members as sources of cognitive conflict or models of behavior from which some rule is observed, abstracted, and later internalized, children may be prepared by evolution to be especially sensitive to group contexts and the social exchanges that occur within them. In one sense, this claim merely moves the explanatory mechanism back one step; we then need to ask how this preparation is activated, and with what outcome. Because these ideas are highly speculative, no easy answer is available. Any answer would probably require a series of studies in which children's competencies in various domains would be assessed in different contexts. In this case, children's competencies in social exchange could be assessed when they are alone and then when they are embedded in groups (for instance, Graziano, Brody, and Bernstein, 1980). If competencies were higher in the group setting, then this outcome would be consistent with the hypothesis.

Conclusion

Social exchange processes may represent a set of basic human social phenomena. The first theories of social exchange focused on basic descriptions of the process. Later, theories expanded to consider proximal mechanisms and, still later, how social exchange processes may change as a result of continuing relationships for the participants. Cognitive elements were introduced to explain the roles of expectations in coordinating social exchanges. With the introduction of cognitive and time perspective factors on social exchange, theories were needed that considered transformational processes. Not incidentally, such transformational processes are central to social development. However, from a developmental perspective, some of the assumptions of social exchange theory appear questionable. For example, is it reasonable to assume that the processes of social exchange are invariant, or at least comparable, for persons in different developmental contexts? Guided by evolutionary theory, we have proposed that factors such as developmental context and genetic relatedness may in fact fundamentally alter social exchange processes. Furthermore, we have explored possible connections among theories of group selection, social exchange, and social development. Ultimately, we have provoked more questions than we have answered, but we hope that this discussion has provided a broader, more textured perspective of the issues at hand.

References

Axelrod, R., and Hamilton, W. D. "The Evolution of Cooperation." *Science,* 1981, *211,* 1390–1396.

Bartholomew, K., and Shaver, P. R. "Methods of Assessing Adult Attachment: Do They Converge?" In J. A. Simpson and W. S. Rholes (eds.), *Attachment Theory and Close Relationships*. New York: Guilford Press, 1998.

Bowlby, J. *Attachment and Loss*, Vol. 1: *Attachment*. New York: Basic Books, 1969.

Bugental, D. B. "Acquisition of the Algorithms of Social Life: A Domain-Based Approach." *Psychological Bulletin*, 2000, *126*, 187–219.

Bugental, D. B., and Goodnow, J. G. "Socialization Processes." In W. Damon (series ed.) and N. Eisenberg (vol. ed.), *Handbook of Child Psychology*, Vol. 3: *Social, Emotional, and Personality Development*. New York: Wiley, 1998.

Buss, D. M. "Evolutionary Psychology: A New Paradigm for Psychological Science." *Psychological Inquiry*, 1995, *6*, 1–49.

Buss, D. M. *The Dangerous Passion*. New York: Free Press, 2000.

Caporael, L. R., and Baron, R. M. "Groups as the Mind's Natural Environment." In J. A. Simpson and D. T. Kenrick (eds.), *Evolutionary Social Psychology*. Mahwah, N.J.: Erlbaum, 1997.

Clark, M. S. "Record Keeping in Two Types of Relationships." *Journal of Personality and Social Psychology*, 1984, *47*, 549–557.

Clark, M. S., and Mills, J. "Interpersonal Attraction in Exchange and Communal Relationships." *Journal of Personality and Social Psychology*, 1979, *37*, 12–24.

Collins, W. A., and Laursen, B. (eds.). *The Minnesota Symposia on Child Psychology*, Vol. 30: *Relationships as Developmental Contexts*. Mahwah, N.J.: Erlbaum, 1999.

Costanzo, P. R. "Morals, Mothers, and Memory: The Social Context of Developing Social Cognition." In R. Cohen and A. W. Siegel (eds.), *Context and Development*. Mahwah, N.J.: Erlbaum, 1991.

Daly, M., Salmon, C., and Wilson, M. "Kinship: The Conceptual Hole in Psychological Studies of Social Cognition and Close Relationships." In J. Simpson and D. T. Kenrick (eds.), *Evolutionary Social Psychology*. Mahwah, N.J.: Erlbaum, 1997.

Darwin, C. *The Descent of Man, and Selection in Relation to Sex*. London: Murray, 1871.

Eisenberg, N. "Emotion, Regulation, and Moral Development." *Annual Review of Psychology*, 2000, *51*, 665–697.

Fiske, A. P. *Structures of Social Life: The Four Elementary Forms of Social Relationships*. New York: Free Press, 1991.

Fiske, A. P. "The Four Elementary Forms of Sociality: Framework for a Unified Theory of Social Relations." *Psychological Review*, 1992, *99*, 689–723.

Foa, E. B., and Foa, U. G. "Resource Theory: Interpersonal Behavior as Exchange." In K. J. Gergen, M. S. Greenberg, and R. H. Willis (eds.), *Social Exchange: Advances in Theory and Research*. New York: Plenum, 1980.

Gergen, K. J. "Toward a Psychology of Receiving Help." *Journal of Applied Social Psychology*, 1974, *4*, 187–193.

Gergen, K. J., Ellsworth, P., Maslach, C., and Seipel, M. "Obligation, Donor Resources, and Reactions to Aid in Three Cultures." *Journal of Personality and Social Psychology*, 1975, *31*, 390–400.

Graziano, W. G. "Standards of Fair Play in Same-Age and Mixed-Age Groups of Children." *Developmental Psychology*, 1978, *14*, 524–530.

Graziano, W. G. "Lost in Thought at the Choice Point: Cognition, Context, and Equity." In J. C. Masters and W. P. Smith (eds.), *Social Comparison, Social Justice, and Relative Deprivation: Theoretical, Empirical, and Policy Perspectives*. Mahwah, N.J.: Erlbaum, 1987.

Graziano, W. G., Brody, G. H., and Bernstein, S. "Effects of Information About Future Interaction and Peer's Motivation on Peer Reward Allocations." *Developmental Psychology*, 1980, *16*, 475–482.

Graziano, W. G., and Tobin, R. M. "Historicity and the Evolution of the Individual Psyche." In D. H. Rosen and M. C. Luebbert (eds.), *Evolution of the Psyche: Human Evolution, Behavior, and Intelligence*. Westport, Conn.: Praeger, 1999.

Haldane, J.B.S. "Population Genetics." *New Biology*, 1955, *18*, 34–51.

Hamilton, W. D. "The Genetical Evolution of Social Behavior: I." *Journal of Theoretical Biology,* 1964a, *7,* 1–16.

Hamilton, W. D. "The Genetical Evolution of Social Behavior: II." *Journal of Theoretical Biology,* 1964b, *7,* 17–52.

Jensen-Campbell, L. A., and Graziano, W. G. "Beyond the Schoolyard: Relationships as Moderators of Daily Interpersonal Conflict." *Personality and Social Psychology Bulletin,* 2000, *26,* 923–935.

Jones, E. E., and Gerard, H. B. *Foundations of Social Psychology.* New York: Wiley, 1967.

Kelley, H. H., and Thibaut, J. W. *Interpersonal Relations: A Theory of Interdependence.* New York: Wiley, 1978.

Lewis, M. "Issues in the Study of Personality Development." *Psychological Inquiry,* 2001, *12,* 67–83.

Lewis, M., Feiring, C., and Rosenthal, S. "Attachment over Time." *Child Development,* 2000, *71,* 707–720.

Maccoby, E. E. "The Uniqueness of the Parent-Child Relationship." In W. A. Collins and B. Laursen (eds.), *The Minnesota Symposia on Child Psychology,* Vol. 30: *Relationships as Developmental Contexts.* Mahwah, N.J.: Erlbaum, 1999.

Nowak, M. A., and Sigmund, K. "Evolution of Indirect Reciprocity by Image Scoring." *Nature,* 1998, *393,* 573–577.

Roberts, G., and Sherratt, T. N. "Development of Cooperative Relationships Through Increasing Investment." *Nature,* 1998, *394,* 175–179.

Sober, E., and Wilson, D. S. *Unto Others: The Evolution and Psychology of Unselfish Behavior.* Cambridge, Mass.: Harvard University Press, 1998.

Thibaut, J. W., and Kelly, H. H. *The Social Psychology of Groups.* New York: Wiley, 1959.

Tooby, J., and Cosmides, L. "The Psychological Foundations of Culture." In J. Barkow, L. Cosmides, and J. Tooby (eds.), *The Adapted Mind: Evolutionary Psychology and the Generation of Culture.* New York: Oxford University Press, 1992.

Trivers, R. L. "The Evolution of Reciprocal Altruism." *Quarterly Review of Biology,* 1971, *46,* 35–57.

Trivers, R. L. "Parent-Offspring Conflict." *American Zoologist,* 1974, *14,* 249–264.

Walster, E., Walster, G. W., and Berscheid, E. *Equity: Theory and Research.* Needham Heights, Mass.: Allyn & Bacon, 1978.

Wilson, D. E. "Incorporating Group Selection into the Adaptationist Program: A Case Study Involving Human Decision Making." In J. A. Simpson and D. T. Kenrick (eds.), *Evolutionary Social Psychology.* Mahwah, N.J.: Erlbaum, 1997.

Wilson, D. E., and Sober, E. "Reintroducing Group Selection to the Human Behavioral Sciences." *Brain and Behavioral Sciences,* 1994, *17,* 585–654.

BRAD E. SHEESE *is a graduate student in the developmental psychology program at Texas A&M University.*

WILLIAM G. GRAZIANO *is professor of psychology at Texas A&M University.*

*This chapter summarizes the ways in which adult men
and women differ in their social exchanges and presents
several theories intended to explain the differences.*

Gender and Social Exchange:
A Developmental Perspective

Eleanor E. Maccoby

My task in this chapter is to consider whether, and how, gender is systematically implicated in social exchanges or interactions. This question necessarily moves us from the level of the individual to the level of dyads or
larger groups. It calls for attention to social contexts and the social structures within which social exchanges occur.

In giving a developmental account of any aspect of behavior, the usual
approach is to start as early in life as possible and then show the changes that
occur in the behavior itself and in the way it is integrated with other aspects
of development as children grow toward adulthood. In this chapter, I proceed
in the reverse way, first describing the ways in which gender is implicated in
adult social exchanges. I outline briefly some of the theories offered to explain
the way gender is enacted in the context of adult social exchanges and then
explore backward to uncover what some of the developmental pathways
might be that lead to the adult outcomes. It may be that this exploration will
call for some modification or amplification in the way theorists have been
interpreting the social exchange behavior of adult men and women.

First, let us note how strongly gender segregation prevails in many contexts of adult life. Even for married couples, the close friends of each member of the couple are largely people of their own sex. Many workplaces are
made up of groups of women doing one kind of work and groups of men
doing another, and these groups are often found in physically separated

Thanks are extended to the following people for providing references for this chapter:
Linda Carli, John Gottman, Campbell Leaper, Deborah Moskowitz, and Cecelia
Ridgeway.

places. Especially in nonprofessional jobs, it is rare to find men and women working side by side at the same kind of work, at the same skill level, and at the same rate of pay. And men and women in the same workplace seldom socialize together. Although the degree of segregation is changing, separation in the workplace remains a fact of life for most working people (Hanson and Pratt, 1995; Reskin and Roos, 1990).

Interactions in Mixed-Sex Task-Oriented Groups

Data on mixed-sex interactions are available from a variety of sources. Here I summarize findings from two: experimental studies and naturalistic studies of the workplace.

Experimental Studies. There is a large body of research in which dyads or groups have been formed for the purpose of studying the distinctive ways in which men and women interact in mixed-sex groups that are engaged in carrying out a task such as solving a problem or resolving a disagreement. Studies done over the past twenty years have yielded a consistent picture:

- In task-oriented groups, people of both sexes concentrate most of their activities on completing the task. In mixed-sex groups, men typically talk more, give more information and opinions, make more task-relevant suggestions, and express more direct disagreement. Women in mixed-sex groups more often express agreement with other speakers, express group solidarity, and adopt a warm, upbeat tone of voice.
- Men have more influence over the task process and outcomes than women do. Indeed, in a mock jury study in which only selected individuals had a piece of important information pertinent to the case under discussion, men and women were equally likely to introduce the information when they possessed it, but it was several times more likely to be used by the group if a man introduced it (Propp, 1995). In general, men in mixed groups do not listen to women as readily as they do to other men, and they are less influenced by female than male coworkers (Tannen, 1994).
- There is some evidence that women do not make strategic use of power, even when they have it, to the same extent that men do (Molm and Hedley, 1992).
- When mixed-sex groups are formed without explicit assignment of authority roles, men tend to emerge as leaders (Eagly and Karau, 1991).
- When interacting with men, women tend to soften their speech. They speak tentatively, as though unsure, and their speech has a polite, deferential quality. Men find women more attractive if they use these softened forms of speech and are more influenced by such women, even though softened speech makes a woman seem less competent (Carli and Eagly, 1999).

- Body language is consistent with verbal behavior. In mixed-sex groups or dyads, men do more chin thrusting and women more smiling and laughing. Men are also more visually dominant; that is, they tend to maintain eye contact with listeners while speaking and disengage visually while listening, whereas women typically do the reverse. These patterns prevail unless a status advantage for women has been explicitly introduced. Women, even strong women who usually use direct gaze while speaking to other women, are more successful in influencing a male partner if they drop their eyes while they themselves are speaking and gaze at their partner when he is speaking (Ellyson, Dovidio, and Brown, 1992).
- Sequential analysis of interchanges in mixed-sex groups has shown that when one member of a task group produces a negative behavior (disagreement, sarcasm, dominant override), men tend to reciprocate with a negative, so that conflict escalates. Women tend not to respond reciprocally to negative inputs from others, but when a group member produces a positive behavior, women tend to reciprocate (Wood and Rhodes, 1992).

How large and generalizable are these gender differences? On this question, experts disagree. Aries (1996, 1998) notes that studies are inconsistent and the magnitude of sex differences usually quite small. In contrast, Carli and Eagly (1999) point to consistent trends across studies. There can be no general answer. Whether the sexes behave differently in groups depends on such matters as the ratio of men to women in the group, what enterprise a group is engaged in, how strong the gender stereotypes are that people bring with them into the group, and whether the context is such as to make gender salient. Interactions among a given group of people change with time, and there is evidence that gender distinctions fade as people become better acquainted.

Workplace Interactions. Many of the findings discussed previously come from elegant experiments with artificially contrived groups of college students. What about task-focused groupings in the real-life world of work? Workplaces are almost always hierarchical, and workers are usually explicitly assigned to a place in the hierarchy. Therefore, many of the studies on the interactions of men and women in the workplace have focused on how the two sexes act in leadership or subordinate positions. In clearly marked authority roles, women and men appear to exercise supervisory responsibilities in much the same way, in the sense that both are mainly concerned with getting the job done; women do not seem more concerned about being liked by their subordinates, as some have predicted. Men and women do not appear to differ in terms of how dominant or directive, or agentic, they are toward their subordinates. But when individuals' authority roles are not clearly marked, stereotypic sex differences emerge in the directiveness of supervisory styles (Molm and Hedley, 1992).

Even when supervisory authority is clear, however, stylistic differences are not entirely absent. Overall, there is a modest tendency for women in leadership positions to be more person oriented (considerate, supportive, appreciative) in their leadership style, but this does not occur at the expense of being effectively directive in getting tasks done. Work by Moskowitz, Suh, and Desauliniers (1994) illustrates this nicely. People at work kept diaries in which they reported each sustained interaction they had with a supervisor, a subordinate, or an equal-status coworker. They described these incidents in terms of how directive or submissive the participant had been toward the coworker and also in terms of communality—that is, how friendly, agreeable, or helpful he or she had been. The directive-submissive behavior turned out to be entirely a function of whether the participant was dealing with a supervisor, a subordinate, or an equal-status coworker. There was no additional influence of gender on directiveness. Women, however, were more likely to incorporate communal elements in their interactions with coworkers.

There are some differences in the way men and women deal with people higher than themselves in the workplace hierarchy. Men appear to be more likely to do favors for a boss, call the boss's attention to something they have accomplished (Tannen, 1994), and to speak about the report of a collaborative project as "my report" rather than "our report."

There are some gendered features of interaction in the workplace that are not captured by the traditional analyses of power relationships or male or female stereotypical personality traits. Johnson (1992) noted that the behavior of both male and female managers toward subordinates depended to some extent on the subordinate's sex. This is not to say that male subordinates were treated as males or female employees as females by both male and female supervisors. Rather, the operative factor was gender sameness. With subordinates of the other sex, managers offered fewer opinions and suggestions, asked more questions, and were more directive than with same-sex subordinates. This was true whether the manager was male or female. The manner of interacting with subordinates of the other sex suggests greater social distance and less easy-going give and take. Greater social ease in the supervisory relationship is experienced on the subordinate's part too. There is reason to believe that as people continue to work with one another over time, they become more comfortable with coworkers of both sexes.

Much has been written about sexual harassment of women in the workplace, usually interpreted as denigration of women and an aspect of male power assertion. But there is another side to sexuality in the workplace. Johnson (1992) speaks of a hidden agenda: the fact that people of both sexes, if they are heterosexual, want to be attractive to persons of the other sex. Group leaders appear to be less task focused when interacting with people of the other sex, perhaps reflecting a secondary agenda that calls for presenting themselves in an attractive light to the other sex, an agenda that may sometimes run counter to the primary agenda of getting the group's work done (Eskilson and Wiley, 1976).

Same-Sex Interaction

Some of the gendered characteristics that are seen in mixed-sex interaction fade away when people are interacting with members of their own sex. In particular, women with other women do not typically soften their speech and body language in the way they do with men (Carli, 1990; Ellyson, Dovidio, and Brown, 1992). Thus, when women interact with others of their own sex, they become more visually dominant than when interacting with men. Men, by contrast, typically employ assertive, direct body language, whether interacting with men or women.

A number of gender discrepancies, however, are maintained or even increased in same-sex interaction. In all-female groups, women devote an even greater proportion of their interactions to socioemotional elements of exchange, displaying more friendliness and mutual helpfulness than is typical in all-male groups. Men are more likely than women to initiate negative acts and to reciprocate another man's negative with a negative of their own, so that conflict escalates (Rhodes and Wood, 1990). Men more often engage in seriously meant oppositional discourse, in which they may highlight their differences and forcefully argue opposed points of view. Women are more likely to soften opposition, to make their views seem more alike rather than more different.

A notable difference between the interactions in all-male compared to all-female groups concerns what people talk about. The informal banter and chatting that goes on in the workplace tends to be sex typed: men talk about sports, cars, sex, and sometimes politics, whereas groups of women having lunch together will typically engage in talk about shopping, clothes, children, and relationships with husbands or boyfriends. Joking and mock insults also appear to be more common among men, whereas women are typically more polite. These divergent interests and styles tend to make same-sex interactions more comfortable and cross-sex interactions more formal and reserved.

Women typically say "I'm sorry" more than men do, and this is true in same-sex as well as cross-sex interactions (Holmes, 1989). Although this might seem to be a form of self-deprecation among women, Tannen (1994) argues that it is better interpreted as a ritual form of politeness, supporting face-saving for a partner by removing implications that the speaker is blaming the partner. This is a ritual that depends on mutuality: one person's apology needs to be followed by the other person's sharing the blame or discounting the need for apology. Tannen (1994) writes, "If one person apologizes and the other simply accepts the apology, then the result is an imbalance—and a loss of face. Many of the rituals typical of women's conversations depend on the goodwill of the other not to take the self-abnegation literally and to restore the balance" (p. 57). In conversations with men, the element of mutual face-saving is more often absent than in conversations among women.

Adult Friendships

There is a qualitative difference between adult male-male friendships and female-female ones. Women spend more time with their same-sex friends than men typically do with theirs, and women's same-sex friendships are more intimate. Through self-disclosure and exchange of information about tastes and personal relationships, women come to know more about each other's lives and give each other more emotional support (Rubin, 1985; Suh and Moskowitz, 1999). Women serve as confidantes for their women friends, whereas men's friends more often serve as companions and as people with whom one exchanges favors and material help. When a man is having problems, his friends usually try to distract him rather than talk about the problem, as women do. In sum, women's same-sex friendships are substantially more intimate than men's (Reis, 1998).

Heterosexual Relationships

The literature on romantic and marital relationships is a rich source of information about gender differences. I focus my review on three areas: intimacy, power, and conflict.

Intimacy. Intimacy, one might expect, must be a two-way street; it is hardly possible to imagine a couple in which one member is closely intimate with the other while the other maintains a more distant relationship. After all, intimacy involves frequent exchange of information and reciprocation of affect. If men and women are accustomed to different levels of intimacy with their same-sex friends, what happens when they enter a close relationship with a lover or spouse? Do they then meet each other halfway, with the woman becoming somewhat more disengaged and the man more closely involved? Or does one adapt more fully than the other to the partner's level?

There may indeed be some asymmetry in intimacy. Although studies are inconsistent, the overall trend is that women disclose their feelings more freely to their male partners than vice versa (Dindia and Allen, 1992). Women also tend to express both positive and negative emotions more openly with their intimate partners than men do and are more adept than men are at reading their partner's emotional signals, such as body language and tone of voice (Hall, 1998).

Of course, self-disclosure and emotional expressiveness are by no means the major processes involved in intimate interactions, and when intimacy is more broadly defined, sex differences largely disappear. Suh and Moskowitz (1999) used diaries of everyday interactions lasting five minutes or more to assess emotional closeness in episodes of interaction with romantic partners as well as with friends. They found that for both men and women, emotional closeness was substantially greater with romantic partners than it was with either same-sex or opposite-sex friends. Notably, men and women reported experiencing equal levels of emotional closeness with their romantic partners. In a study of heterosexual couples in their late twenties and early thirties (Reis, Lin, Bennett, and Newlek, 1993), men and women also reported equal levels of intimacy with their spouses or significant others.

We do not see a picture of two people with different dispositions meeting each other halfway. Rather, it appears that men are fully as capable as women of intimacy in interaction with another person when that person is a woman in a close relationship. With male friends, many men appear to put up barriers of some kind—or perhaps heterosexual men do not find that a relationship with a male friend is the right context for intimacy.

The Balance of Power. We turn now to the question of whether there is any overall pattern of male privilege or dominance in the social exchanges that occur between heterosexual couples, as there is in the world of work. If this were so, we would expect women to be the more deferential, more accommodating, and less assertive member of the couple in both speech and action. But between the members of a heterosexual couple, matters of power and subordination are being enacted in a very different context than is the case for coworkers. The sexual bond raises the level of intensity of their emotions in relation to each other. There can be intense conflict, but their emotional bonding implies mutual empathy and a readiness by each to try to please the other and act in the interests of the other. And when couples marry or begin to live together, their daily lives become more closely intertwined, and they take on a joint agenda having to do with maintaining and managing a household. For many couples, rearing children becomes an added agenda. There is usually a division of labor such that each takes responsibility for certain household and family tasks, thus reducing the occasions when negotiation is required and giving each partner power to make certain kinds of decisions affecting the partnership. All of these considerations mean that the question of who has more authority in the relationship may fade into the background in most daily social exchanges.

What can be said concerning the balance of power between men and women in intimate relationships? As Huston (1983) noted, power in the relationship between intimate partners can come from a number of sources: which person has more information, which has more financial resources, which has more publicly legitimized authority, and which is more in love (the person less in love has more power). In traditional societies, husbands clearly have greater publicly legitimized authority, and this can be a controlling factor in the balance of power (although in the privacy of the home, women can be the primary decision makers, even in traditional societies). But in modern Western societies, the many facets of power can balance out, and it may become impossible to say that one person has more overall power than the other.

Huston and Ashmore (1986) describe some of the same interactional characteristics that we have already noted in the workplace or between friends: that women do more of the work involved in keeping a partner in a positive mood and are more supportive of their partner's speaking than men are in relation to their women partners. A more recent study (Robey, Canary, and Burggraf, 1998) found that wives devote somewhat more energy to maintaining conversations by such means as asking questions, but there was no overall pattern of dominance; husbands and wives typically talked equally often, and neither interrupted more. Although women's tendency to support a male partner's conversation has sometimes been interpreted as a sign of women's subordinate status, we should note that women are supportive of a partner's speech when interacting with their women friends and even with children (Maccoby, 1998), circumstances that can hardly be seen as subordination to a dominant partner.

Regarding the question of whether the pattern within heterosexual couples is one of male dominance, Suh and Moskowitz (1998) report relevant data in a study of same-sex friendships, cross-sex friendships, and married or cohabiting couples. Working with diaries of interaction events, these researchers assessed agency displayed by each participant, where agency reflected the ratio of dominance to submission in interactions. Men in this study displayed more agency than did women in interaction with friends. In interactions with spouses, women displayed somewhat more dominance and less submission than men. The authors do not tell us how long these couples had been together, which may be crucial, but on the basis of this study and those reviewed above, we can see that there is no general answer to the question of which sex is dominant in heterosexual couples. For many couples, dominance is hardly relevant, and it becomes less so over time as the partners shift into a communal pursuit of a joint agenda. For others, dominance issues may be confined to a few domains. In one small-scale study of couples married at least ten years (Walker, 1996), both husbands and wives agreed that when they watched television together, the husband dominated control of the remote control device, and wives expressed considerable frustration over not being able to see the programs of their own choice (except, perhaps, by taping them and viewing them later). This work alerts us to the possibility that existing studies may have underrepresented domains in which dominance issues plague domestic couples. Of course, there may have been secular change such that dominance relationships between older couples are quite different from those between young people. One thing we have not seen so far is a consistent pattern of male privilege in the interactions of intimate couples in modern Western societies.

Marital Conflict. One might expect that studies of male and female roles in marital conflict would focus largely on who wins when the interests of husbands and wives conflict and who is more adaptable in adopting the other's objectives or point of view. But the realities of marital conflict are more complex. Gottman and Notarius (2000) have noted how elusive the dynamics of power within couples can be when researchers attempt to observe and measure the exercise of power during marital conflicts. Rather, affect and its regulation between members of a couple (specifically, the extent to which one or both of the partners work to soothe the male) are of great importance in the outcome of marital conflicts. Affect regulation appears to be more important than the content of a quarrel and cannot be easily understood in terms of dominance-submission or win-lose patterns.

A dimension of marital conflict that has consistently emerged is that women "nag" and men turn passive or distant and try to avoid becoming engaged with their wives in a problem-solving discussion that might be conflictual. Gottman and Levinson (1988) concluded that wives tend to remain engaged in a conflict with their husbands, and even be coercive toward them, whereas men are more likely to try to pacify women, withdraw, or stonewall. Christensen and Heavey (1990) have studied what they call the demand-withdrawal interaction pattern, in which one partner tries to discuss problems, criticizes and blames the partner for the problems, and requests or demands change, while the other partner tries to avoid discussion of the problems, defends self against the criticisms, and withdraws from the discussion. They have used both self-report and observational measures and consistently find that women are more likely to be the ones who do the demanding and criticizing and men the withdrawing. There is a good deal of unpleasant affect for both parties in encounters of this kind. Suh and Moskowitz (1999) report greater intensity of unpleasant affect between heterosexual partners than between either cross-sex or same-sex friends. But they also report that in interactions with their partners, men were more agreeable, on the average, and less quarrelsome, than were women, and when conflict escalates into violence, women are at least as likely as men to yell, hit, or throw objects at their partners (Moffitt, Caspi, Rutter, and Silva, forthcoming).

Why does the pattern of female demanding and nagging and male withdrawing and stonewalling occur? Several possibilities have been offered. Gottman and Levinson (1988) have found (using physiological measures) that men become more emotionally aroused during marital conflicts than women do and that high arousal occurs more rapidly. They suggest that men find it difficult to tolerate this high level of negative arousal and try to shut it down by stonewalling. There are additional possibilities. One is that men are inhibited about using the kind of confrontational tactics with their wives that they have been accustomed to using in conflicts with men, while at the same time being less skilled in negotiation and talking about conflict (Maccoby, 1998). It has also been suggested (Sagrestano, Heavey, and Christensen, 1998) that women are more often in a position of needing to make demands on their husbands than vice versa—for example, demands for money and for help with household and child care tasks—a situation that fosters male withdrawal. When husbands need to make demands on their wives, wives do more withdrawing than they do when it is they themselves who want to influence their partner's behavior. Nonetheless, even when the effect of which partner wants change has been accounted for, there remains a substantial tendency for husbands to do more withdrawing and wives to do more demanding and nagging.

In a recent review, Sagristano, Heavey, and Christensen (1998) note that women typically want more intimacy, more time together, and more sharing of feelings in marriage than men do. Men, by contrast, want more privacy and more time alone. The researchers find that when a couple is asymmetrical in these respects, they are more likely to display the demand-withdrawal syndrome. The partner who derives satisfaction from being alone is the one who withdraws during conflict. What remains to be explained is why many women should want more intimacy in marriage than their husbands do.

Explanatory Theories: Their Fit with the Data

We consider now some of the theories that have been brought to bear on the gendered patterns of adult social interaction.

Social Exchange Theory. A dominant theme in the work of sociologists is that sex differences in workplace behavior reflect differential positions of men and women in the power structures where working lives take place. The basic idea is that persons higher in a power structure control more resources and that persons lower in the power structure not only value and need these resources, but have few alternative means of acquiring them. In social exchange theory, lower-status people must exchange something of value with those in the hierarchy above them. They must not only perform the work for which they are being paid but must also adapt themselves to the requirements and control of the more powerful persons. People with lesser power may be expected to show deference toward powerful persons not only by complying with their demands but through body language, tones of voice, and nonassertive speech. A simple social exchange theory model (Kanter, 1977) would predict that sex differences in interactive behavior should disappear when the objective level of power is equated. As we have seen, this seems to happen with respect to agentic or directive interaction styles but not with respect to the socioemotional realm of interaction.

Status Theories of Power. These models do not hold that equating objective power will erase sex differences in interactive behavior. Rather, proponents of this theory argue that males have greater status and greater prestige than women do, over and above whatever prestige may accrue to their objective position in a power structure. In many societies, status is conferred on males through a variety of formal and informal means, such as greater legal rights to vote or hold property or divorce a spouse or such customs as serving food to men before women and children can eat. In the language of status theory, sex (or gender) is a diffuse status characteristic. The claim is that people of both sexes will accord higher status to a male than to a female partner on the basis of gender alone. Men, in enacting a given role, do so from the assumption that they have greater power and prestige, and this affects the confidence and assertiveness with which they carry out the functions required by the role (Ridgeway and Diekema, 1992).

In an elaboration of status theory, expectation states theory holds that men's greater status carries with it a set of assumptions that in the absence of specific information to the contrary causes the members of a group to expect that the males will have more knowledge and more competence to bring to bear on the group's activities than females do. Therefore, male members of a group will be given more opportunities to speak, will be listened to more carefully, and will have more influence on group process. Evidence from both laboratory and workplace studies confirms this prediction, at least in the initial stages of a group's interaction. When a woman does in fact have greater knowledge or expertise on matters relevant to the group's task, this fact has to be made very explicit to the other members of the group before it weakens their assumptions and allows gender-neutral interaction styles to emerge.

Social exchange and status theories of power are primarily concerned with understanding the ways men and women behave in mixed-sex situations within various power structures. They have had less to say about the ways men and women interact with others of their own sex. Because there is no power gradient based on sex in same-sex groups, there appears to be no reason that women in their groups should behave any differently from men in theirs, and status theories would predict that men and women would be more alike in their social interaction styles when they are in same-sex groups than when they are interacting with people of the other sex.

As we have seen, the evidence on this issue is mixed, but the prediction is largely disconfirmed. Women in their groups appear to be equally agentic with men in theirs but different when it comes to the socioemotional realm. It is true that when it comes to body language, tentative speech, and smiling or laughing, women soften their behavior less in all-female situations than when men are present. On the whole, however, many aspects of women's distinctive interaction styles are maintained or even strengthened in all-female groups. This is especially the case with the mutually supportive socioemotional elements in interaction. Among men, boldness and toughness are especially likely to be displayed to a male audience in male groups or dyads. These distinctive behaviors can hardly be a function of a gendered power gradient in the immediate context. Exchange and status theories fail when it comes to accounting for these things, as they do in accounting for the qualitative differences between male-male and female-female friendships.

Social Role Theory. Eagly has proposed a social role theory that seeks to explain the way men and women behave in groups, whether or not the group includes members of both sexes (Carli and Eagly, 1999; Eagly, 1987). The theory is based on the sexual division of labor that has long characterized most societies, with women being predominantly involved in child care and household management and men in breadwinning in the larger world outside the family. Despite recent rapid changes in sex roles, a good deal of the traditional division of labor between the sexes still prevails. Eagly holds that people adapt themselves to the requirements of these differentiated roles, seeking to acquire the knowledge and skills needed for them and modifying their social behavior in line with these differentiated roles. Thus, women, because of their functions in the care of children and the elderly, become more attuned to the needs and emotional states of others, more nurturant, more willing to subordinate their own immediate interests for the sake of others, and more concerned with maintaining harmony. In short, female roles call for communal characteristics. Men, by contrast, work in competitive environments and often have work roles requiring initiative, independence, and agentic characteristics.

According to the theory, women carry over into the workplace and other out-of-home settings these other-oriented, nurturant tendencies; that is, they suppress aggression and display cooperative and conciliatory behavior. These adaptations are thought to be fairly pervasive in that they come to characterize a woman's behavior in a variety of settings, regardless of whether she is interacting with men or with other women and regardless of her position in a power structure. They come to be embodied in widely held stereotypes concerning behaviors expected from people of the two sexes, and they become normative in that they embody beliefs concerning what behaviors are right and proper for men and women. According to Carli and Eagly (1999), "To the extent that these normative expectations about behavior appropriate to women and men become internalized as part of individuals' self-concepts and personalities, people form dispositions or traits that are consistent with gender roles" (p. 8). Thus, when a woman is placed in a managerial position that would call for agentic behavior, one should still expect to see that she would be more likely than a man in a similar job to avoid confrontation and be more supportive of coworkers and cooperative in the way she enacts her occupational role. It is with respect to the formation of individually internalized gendered dispositions or traits that this theory diverges most clearly from the power and status theories.

Social role theory deals nicely with the fact that men and women have interaction styles that differ in some respects, whether they are in same-sex or mixed-sex groups. It encompasses the differences in male as compared with female same-sex friendships and also the different interests the two sexes display in their informal same-sex conversations. It also describes why it is the female in a heterosexual pair who more often works to sustain conversations, create positive moods, and more skillfully read a partner's body language. It has more difficulty, however, with the fact that people behave differently depending on the sex of the person with whom they are interacting. It is not clear what to expect from this theory for male-female encounters. Presumably, each would carry into such encounters the habitual sex-typed personality traits derived from social roles. This could mean disjunction and awkwardness in interaction and mutual misunderstandings, or it could mean that each adapts to the other by adjusting his or her own behavior in the partner's direction, so that women would become more agentic and men more empathic or communal when interacting with a partner of the other sex. In fact, this pattern of meeting the other halfway does not appear to describe what actually happens. When women soften their speech in talking with men, they are not becoming more like men. And when members of a heterosexual pair become equally emotionally close, this appears to happen because men have made the greater change, matching or even exceeding their partner's initial capacity for intimacy.

Indeed, all three of the theories discussed so far have difficulty dealing with some of the major themes that have emerged from my review:

• None of the theories attempts to deal focally with the degree of gender segregation that prevails in workplaces and many social situations.

• Much that happens in social exchanges depends not on the sex of the actor or the sex of the partner, but on the match between the two. There is a comfort factor in same-sex interactions. And certain interaction patterns are found primarily in all-male or all-female settings. For example, males bring out elements of rivalry and daring in one another that are seldom elicited in them by women or elicited in women by men.

• The theories are anemic in that they have little to say about the strong force of heterosexual attraction. We noted the hidden agenda that surfaces in mixed-sex task-focused groups: both men and women strive to be seen as attractive by people of the other sex. Although women's tendency to soften their speech and body language when interacting with men has been interpreted as a form of bowing to men's greater status, it could alternatively be seen as a means of gaining men's attention and compliance using sexual attraction.

• Men's ability to achieve emotional closeness with romantic partners (and to a lesser extent with women friends) while such closeness is warded off in interactions among males is a powerful phenomenon that calls for explanation.

• I have noted a pattern in heterosexual couples in which the woman complains and nags and the man withdraws or stonewalls. This pattern remains only partially explained as a matter of men's greater control of resources. If indeed it also reflects a greater need that women have for emotional closeness, the theories described so far do not offer explanations.

We now turn to a developmental perspective to see whether it can bring additional explanatory power to the theories discussed so far.

The Developmental Perspective

Developmental theorists have been concerned with explaining sex differences in terms of their childhood origins. They have stressed not only the childhood conditions that would cause boys and girls to differ with respect to sex-typed traits, but also those that bring about individual variation within each sex with respect to how masculine or feminine a boy or girl becomes. Traditional theories have been dispositional, in that they have assumed that certain sex-typed tendencies are laid down in childhood and become internalized, becoming reasonably (though not totally) stable by the time adulthood is reached.

Psychodynamic Theories. Psychodynamic theories pointed to the dynamics of relationships with parents as the wellspring from which gender identity and sex typing of personality characteristics emerge. Although Freud's original theory differentiating the sexes in terms of their different oedipal experiences in childhood has been considerably modified in the light of more recent empirical findings (for example, Friedman and Downey, 1995), psychodynamic views stressing the importance of early parent-child bonds and identifications continue to be influential among feminist theorists.

Cognitive Developmental Theories. Cognitive developmentalists have stressed the acquisition of gender stereotypes and gender schemas, which serve as selective filters for incoming information and as a basis for children's own efforts to conform to what they see as appropriate for children of their own sex.

Social Learning Theories. Social learning theory emphasizes the real-life consequences of behaving in ways that are appropriate or inappropriate according to the social standards for each sex. This theory also emphasizes the importance of modeling, in which children conform to the norm of the multiple exemplars of sex-differentiated behaviors presented by a variety of available models. Bussey and Bandura's (1999) social cognitive theory gives, in addition, an important role to children's active selection and construction of the environments to which they will be exposed and children's self-regulation through self-imposed sanctions.

The Two Cultures Theory. Without implying that other socialization settings are unimportant, this theory focuses on one in particular: the childhood peer group. It points to the well-documented and robust tendency for children from about age four to about age twelve to separate into same-sex groups and choose same-sex friends. Demonstrably different interaction styles develop in all-male as compared to all-female children's groups. The theory holds that styles are internalized by individual boys and girls, becoming not only part of their habitual behavioral repertoire but also sustained by group norms that make these interaction styles seem correct and expected. When children grow older and begin to interact more with people of the other sex, they tend to display the interaction styles they adopted at an earlier time in their same-sex groups. Differences in the male and female styles will lead to awkward and disrupted interactions in which expected reciprocations may not occur.

Maltz and Borker (1982) were among the first to articulate this account of cross-gender miscommunication. They argued that neither a power differential nor basic personality differences between the sexes were required to give rise to the different interactive styles. More recently, Tannen (1990, 1994) provided detailed examples of miscommunication between men and women that do seem to stem from habitual differences in their interactive styles. It is evident that the greater comfort that men and women seem to feel with others of their own sex in the workplace is predictable from having spent so much of their unstructured out-of-home time as children with same-sex playmates.

In recent years, a two cultures theory has been both elaborated and modified. Considerable effort has been directed toward understanding why children segregate by sex in the first place (Leaper, 1994; Maccoby, 1998; Maccoby and Jacklin, 1987) and documenting the ways in which the cultures of male and female groups do and do not differ. It is widely acknowledged that individual children may have very different experiences within a same-sex group. It has also become evident, however, that groups have characteristics that individuals do not and that it is worthwhile to study the characteristics and processes of male and female groups, over and above the characteristics of the individuals and their roles within the group. The predominant characteristics of male and female children's groups and of same-sex friendships have been fully described elsewhere (Maccoby 1998, 2000; Ruble and Martin, 1998). Suffice it to say that there are strong parallels between the gendered interaction patterns seen in childhood and the adult patterns already summarized in this chapter—for example,

- Gender segregation is strongly present in childhood contexts not structured by adults, from preschool into adolescence.
- Girls' friendships are typically more intimate than boys' friendships.
- Boys, in their groups, are more competitive, more concerned than girls in their groups with issues of status and dominance, and more wary about showing signs of weakness to other males.
- Boys are considerably more likely to engage in group enterprises in pursuit of group goals (Benenson, Apostoleris, and Parnass, 1997), and it has been suggested that in this way they achieve greater collective power than girls do in their group activities (Maccoby, 2000).
- In same-sex task-oriented groups or dyads, the two sexes are equally concerned with doing the task well, but girls have an additional agenda of maintaining group harmony. As a consequence, their discourse is more reciprocal and more collaborative.
- In middle childhood, the interests of the two sexes diverge sharply. Girls are more interested in domestic, romantic, and human-relational themes, and these interests show themselves in their preferences for reading matter and television programs, as well as in their imaginative play with other girls. The fantasies, play, and television preferences of young boys involve themes of danger, acts of bravery, and combat with enemies. In middle

childhood, these games often metamorphose into team sports. The content of conversations among boys is typically quite different from that among girls, and children sometimes note that they do not know what to say to children of the other sex.

We see that there are compelling continuities from childhood to adulthood with regard to gender segregation and the importance of the gender composition of dyads or groups. There are continuities, too, in aspects of interaction style and in the interests and agendas that members of same-sex groups share. It is interesting that women in positions of official authority are reported not to use their power to the same extent that men in authority typically do, possibly an echo of the greater use of collective power by boys' groups in childhood. I argue that the two cultures perspective fills some of the explanatory gaps left by the theories of adult gendered patterns of social exchange. If sex-distinctive patterns that were already operating in childhood are seen in adulthood, it does not make sense to interpret the adult patterns entirely in terms of adult context, such as power dynamics in the workplace or the assignment of adult men and women to divergent roles in breadwinning or child rearing. Rather, attention to developmental histories is needed.

Predictions from childhood to adults' interactions with same-sex others are relatively straightforward, and we have seen that in a number of respects, the match is quite good. Predicting from what happens in childhood same-sex encounters to what will happen in adult cross-sex encounters is much less straightforward. We can see that distinctive male and female styles might be expected to lead to miscommunication and frustration in achieving mutuality of influence between adult men and women. We have seen evidence that this is indeed the case. But in adolescence and adulthood, the powerful forces of sexuality introduce a new agenda. Insofar as childhood peer group socialization deals with sexuality at all, it appears to take the form, in girls, of interpreting cross-sex attraction in romantic terms, whereas among boys, such attraction is more typically interpreted in specifically sexual terms. In a recent modification of two cultures theory, Maccoby (1998) notes that the introduction of sexuality into the cross-sex equation means that male-female relations and modes of exchange need to be reconstructed, not simply carried over or adapted from earlier same-sex modes of interaction. It means that the balance of power between men and women in close relationships can be quite different from what prevails in other contexts. We have seen that women are capable of expressing more direct aggression toward an intimate male partner than toward others. We have also seen in men a different pattern of intimate and emotionally close interaction with a heterosexual partner than is seen in their relationships with other males, in either childhood or adulthood. A developmental perspective, then, does not promise simple continuities. It does have something to say, however, about the fund of sex-distinctive earlier experience that adults bring to their interpersonal negotiations in adult contexts and about the ways in which gender matters as these negotiations are carried out.

References

Aries, E. *Men and Women in Interaction: Reconsidering the Differences.* New York: Oxford University Press, 1996.

Aries, E. "Gender Differences in Interaction." In D. J. Canary and K. Dindia (eds.), *Sex Differences and Similarities in Communication.* Mahwah, N.J.: Erlbaum, 1998.

Benenson, J. F., Apostoleris, N. H., and Parnass, J. "Age and Sex Differences in Dyadic and Group Interaction." *Developmental Psychology,* 1997, *33,* 538–543.

Bussey, K., and Bandura, A. "Social Cognitive Theory of Gender Development and Differentiation." *Psychological Review,* 1999, *106,* 676–713.

Carli, L. L. "Gender, Language, and Influence." *Journal of Personality and Social Psychology,* 1990, *59,* 941–951.

Carli, L. L., and Eagly, A. H. "Gender Effects on Social Influence and Emergent Leadership." In G. Powell (ed.), *Gender in Organizations.* Thousand Oaks, Calif.: Sage, 1999.

Christensen, A., and Heavey, C. L. "Gender Differences in Marital Conflict: The Demand-Withdrawal Interaction Pattern." In S. Oskamp and M. Constanzo (eds.), *Gender Issues in Contemporary Society.* Thousand Oaks, Calif.: Sage, 1990.

Dindia, K., and Allen, M. "Sex Differences in Self-Disclosure: A Meta Analysis." *Psychological Bulletin,* 1992, *112,* 106–124.

Eagly, A. H. *Sex Differences in Social Behavior: A Social Role Interpretation.* Mahwah, N.J.: Erlbaum, 1987.

Eagly, A. H., and Karau, S. J. "Gender and the Emergence of Leaders: A Meta-Analysis." *Journal of Personality and Social Psychology,* 1991, *60,* 685–710.

Ellyson, S. L., Dovidio, J. F., and Brown, C. E. "The Look of Power: Gender Differences and Similarities in Visual Dominance Behavior." In C. L. Ridgeway (ed.), *Gender, Interaction and Inequality.* New York: Springer-Verlag, 1992.

Eskilson, A., and Wiley, M. G. "Sex Composition and Leadership in Small Groups." *Sociometry,* 1976, *39,* 183–194.

Friedman, R. C., and Downey, J. I. "Biology and the Oedipus Complex." *Psychoanalytic Quarterly,* 1995, *64,* 234–264.

Gottman, J. M., and Levinson, R. W. "The Social Psychophysiology of Marriage." In P. Noller and M. Fitzpatrick (eds.), *Perspectives on Marital Interaction.* Philadelphia: Multilingual Matters, 1988.

Gottman, J. M., and Notarius, C. I. "Decade Review: Observing Marital Interaction." *Journal of Marriage and the Family,* 2000, *62,* 927–947.

Hall, J. A. "How Big Are Nonverbal Sex Differences? The Case of Smiling and Sensitivity to Nonverbal Cues." In D. J. Canary and K. Dindia (eds.), *Sex Differences and Similarities in Communication.* Mahwah, N.J.: Erlbaum, 1998.

Hanson, S., and Pratt, G. *Gender, Work and Space.* New York: Routledge, 1995.

Holmes, J. "Sex Differences in Apologies: One Aspect of Communicative Competence." *Applied Linguistics,* 1989, *10,* 194–213.

Huston, T. L. "Power." In H. H. Kelley and others (eds.), *Close Relationships.* New York: Freeman, 1983.

Huston, T. L., and Ashmore, R. D. "Women and Men in Personal Relationships." In R. D. Ashmore and R. K. DelBoca (eds.), *The Social Psychology of Male-Female Relations.* Orlando, Fla.: Academic Press, 1986.

Johnson, C. "Gender, Formal Authority and Leadership." In C. L. Ridgeway (ed.), *Gender, Interaction and Inequality.* New York: Springer-Verlag, 1992.

Kanter, R. *Men and Women of the Corporation.* New York: Basic Books, 1977.

Leaper, C. (ed.). *Childhood Gender Segregation: Causes and Consequences*. New Directions for Child Development, no. 65. San Francisco: Jossey-Bass, 1994.

Maccoby, E. E. *The Two Sexes: Growing Up Apart, Coming Together*. Cambridge, Mass.: Harvard University Press, 1998.

Maccoby, E. E. "Perspectives on Gender Development." *International Journal of Behavioral Development*, 2000, *24*, 398–406.

Maccoby, E. E., and Jacklin, C. N. "Gender Segregation in Childhood." In H. Reese (ed.), *Advances in Child Development and Behavior*. Orlando, Fla.: Academic Press, 1987.

Maltz, D. N., and Borker, R. A. "A Cultural Approach to Male-Female Miscommunication." In J. J. Gumperz (ed.), *Language and Social Identity*. New York: Cambridge University Press, 1982.

Moffitt, T. E., Caspi, A., Rutter, M., and Silva, P. A. *Sex Differences in Antisocial Behaviour: Conduct Disorder, Delinquency and Violence in the Duneeden Longitudinal Study*. Cambridge: Cambridge University Press, forthcoming.

Molm, L. D., and Hedley, M. "Gender, Power and Social Exchange." In C. L. Ridgeway (ed.), *Gender, Interaction and Inequality*. New York: Springer-Verlag, 1992.

Moskowitz, D. S., Suh, E. J., and Desauliniers, J. "Situational Influences on Gender Differences in Agency and Communion." *Journal of Personality and Social Psychology*, 1994, *66*, 753–761.

Propp, K. M. "An Experimental Examination of Biological Sex as a Status Cue in Decision-Making Groups and Its Influence in Information Use." *Small Group Research*, 1995, *26*, 451–474.

Reis, H. T. "Gender Differences in Intimacy and Related Behaviors: Context and Process." In D. J. Canary and K. Dindia (eds.), *Sex Differences and Similarities in Communication*. Mahwah, N.J.: Erlbaum, 1998.

Reis, H. T., Lin, Y. C., Bennett, E. S., and Newlek, J. "Change and Consistency in Social Participation During Early Adulthood." *Developmental Psychology*, 1993, *29*, 633–645.

Reskin, B. F., and Roos, P. *Job Queues and Gender Queues: Explaining Women's Inroads into Male Occupations*. Philadelphia: Temple University Press, 1990.

Rhodes, N., and Wood, W. "Sequences of Interaction Among Males and Females in Task Groups." Unpublished manuscript, Texas A&M University, 1990.

Ridgeway, C. L., and Diekema, D. "Are Gender Differences Status Differences?" In C. L. Ridgeway (ed.), *Gender, Interaction and Inequality*. New York: Springer-Verlag, 1992.

Robey, E. B., Canary, D. J., and Burggraf, C. S. "Conversational Maintenance Behaviors of Husbands and Wives: An Observational Analysis." In D. J. Canary and K. Dindia (eds.), *Sex Differences and Similarities in Communication*. Mahwah, N.J.: Erlbaum, 1998.

Rubin, L. B. *Just Friends: The Role of Friendship in Our Lives*. New York: HarperCollins, 1985.

Ruble, D. N., and Martin, C. L. "Gender Development." In W. Damon (series ed.) and N. Eisenberg (vol. ed.), *Handbook of Child Psychology*, Vol. 3: *Social, Emotional, and Personality Development*. New York: Wiley, 1998.

Sagrestano, L. M., Heavey, C. L., and Christensen, A. "Theoretical Approaches to Understanding Sex Differences and Similarities in Conflict Behavior." In D. J. Canary and K. Dindia (eds.), *Sex Differences and Similarities in Communication*. Mahwah, N.J.: Erlbaum, 1998.

Suh, E. J., and Moskowitz, D. S. "Relationship Influences on Gender Differences in Agency and Communion." Paper presented at the annual meeting of the American Psychological Association, San Francisco, Aug. 1998.

Suh, E. J., and Moskowitz, D. S. "Personal Relationship Influences on Affect and Intimacy." Paper presented at the annual meeting of the American Psychological Association, Boston, Aug. 1999.

Tannen, D. *You Just Don't Understand: Women and Men in Conversation*. New York: Morrow, 1990.

Tannen, D. *Talking from 9 to 5: How Women's and Men's Conversational Styles Affect Who Gets Heard, Who Gets Credit, and What Gets Done at Work.* New York: Morrow, 1994.

Walker, A. J. "Couples Watching Television: Gender, Power, and the Remote Control." *Journal of Marriage and the Family,* 1996, *58,* 813–823.

Wood, W., and Rhodes, N. "Sex Differences in Interactive Styles in Task Groups." In C. L. Ridgeway (ed.), *Gender, Interaction and Inequality.* New York: Springer-Verlag, 1992.

ELEANOR E. MACCOBY is emeritus professor of psychology at Stanford University.

Name Index

Aber, J. L., 20
Aboud, F. E., 36
Ainsworth, M.D.S., 19, 20
Allen, M., 92
Amazeen, P. G., 53, 58, 60, 65, 67
Anderson, D., 17
Apostoleris, N. H., 101
Aquan-Assee, J., 10
Archer, R. L., 9
Aries, E., 89
Arnett, J. J., 69
Aron, A., 61, 65
Aron, E. N., 61, 65
Aronson, E., 55
Arrow, H., 58
Asch, S. E., 63
Ashmore, R. D., 93
Axelrod, R., 79

Bagwell, C. L., 35
Baillargeon, R., 36
Bak, P., 59
Baldwin, M. W., 29
Bales, R. F., 54
Bandura, A., 1, 100
Bardahl, J. L., 58
Baron, R. M., 53, 55, 56, 58, 60, 62, 65, 67, 82
Barrett, K., 14
Bartholomew, K., 75
Baumeister, R. F., 28
Baumrind, D., 46
Beek, P. J., 53, 58, 60, 65, 67
Behan, A., 5
Benenson, J. F., 101
Bennett, E. S., 93
Berg, J. H., 9
Berndt, T. J., 15, 30, 36
Bernstein, S., 35, 83
Berscheid, E. S., 1, 30, 41, 44, 76, 77, 78
Betts, N. T., 36
Bigelow, B. J., 27, 31, 33
Billman, J., 35
Birch, L. L., 35
Bjerstadt, A., 17
Blaney, N., 55
Blehar, M. C., 19, 20
Borker, R. A., 100

Bowlby, J., 14, 19, 75
Brody, G. H., 35, 83
Bromley, D. B., 31
Brown, C. E., 91
Brownell, C. A., 27
Buber, M., 62, 68
Bugental, D. B., 14, 28, 31, 75, 77
Bukowski, W. M., 10, 19, 28, 31
Burggraf, C. S., 93–94
Burns, A. A., 31
Buss, D., 17, 75, 79
Buss, L. W., 56, 60
Bussey, K., 100
Buunk, B. P., 12

Cairns, R. B., 1
Campbell, D. T., 58–59
Campos, J. J., 14
Campos, R., 14
Canary, D. J., 93–94
Caporael, L. R., 53, 55, 56, 62, 82
Carli, L. L., 88, 89, 91, 97, 98
Caspi, A., 95
Cassidy, J., 19
Cerreto, M., 12
Chaiken, A. L., 14
Chao, C., 36
Chen, X., 20
Chomsky, N., 31, 36, 43, 44
Chrisman, K., 7
Christensen, A., 95, 96
Christensen, L., 10
Cicchetti, D., 20
Clark, M., 3, 4–5, 7, 8, 9, 10, 11, 17, 29, 31, 34, 35, 54, 62, 74, 78
Clary, E. G., 19
Cohen, S., 8
Coie, J. D., 20
Colby, A., 46
Collins, N. L., 8, 10
Collins, W. A., 30
Cook, T. D., 35
Coppotelli, H., 20
Corcoran, D., 4–5
Cosmides, L., 28, 75
Costanzo, P., 41–42, 46, 74, 77
Crick, N. R., 20
Cummings, E. M., 19
Cutrona, C. E., 8

107

Subject Index

Affect, 50
Altruism, 7
Attachment, 19, 20–21
Attractors, 63, 64, 65, 66, 68
Authoritative parents, 46

Belonging, need for, 28
Benefits: in close relationships, 11; of communal norms, 11; in communal relationships, 4, 29; comparison and, 76–77; costs of, 5–7; definition of, 3; donors of, 3; evolutionary theory and, 79; in exchange relationships, 29; group selection and, 82; of mother-child relationship, 78; recipients of, 3

Catastrophe flags, 55
Child abuse, 20
Children: attachment and, 19, 20–21; chores and, 15; communal norms and, 14–16; distributive justice norms and, 16–18; empathy and, 14; external reinforcement and, 1; gender segregation and, 99–103; learning of, 1; moral internalization and, 46–49; need for belonging, 28; notions of reciprocity and, 31; parenting styles and, 46; parent-offspring conflict and, 80; peer relationships and, 15, 16; prosocial behavior and, 19; rejection and, 20; relationship with mothers, 75, 77–78; relationship with parents, 14–16; role models and, 15; self-interest of, 16
Chores, 15
Closed-field settings, 36–37
Coalitions, 66, 67
Cognitive developmental theories, 100
Cohesiveness, 58, 59
Communal norms: application of, 9; attachment and, 19, 20–21; benefits of, 11; child abuse and, 20; children and, 14–16; in close relationships, 8–9; developmental differences and, 14–16; in exchange relationships, 13–14; fortitudes for, 9–11; mood and, 5; parents and, 14–16; patterns of adherence to, 11–12; personality traits and, 11; potential donors and, 3; potential recipients and, 3; preference

for, 8–9; prosocial behavior and, 19; recipients and, 3; role models and, 15; self-interest and, 8–9, 16; social skills for, 9–11; stress and, 11; trust and, 11–12
Communal relationships: altruism and, 7; benefits in, 4, 29; child development and, 34, 35–36; chores and, 15; cost of benefits of, 5–7, 9; distributive justice norms and, 17–18; duration of, 7; versus exchange relationships, 4–7; interdependence and, 54–55; motivation for, 7; overview of, 29; repayments and, 4; strength of, 5–7; studies of, 4–5. *See also* Dynamical systems
Communal strength, 5–7
Community development, 60–61
Comparison Level of Alternatives, 61, 68, 76
Competition, 36, 37
Complementary reciprocity, 30
Cooperation, 55
Costs: of communal relationships, 5–7, 9; comparison and, 76–77; evolutionary theory and, 79; group selection and, 82; of marriage, 9; of mother-child relationships, 78

Dating relationships, 8–9, 10
Deep structures, 31–32, 43
Demand-withdrawal interaction pattern, 95–96
Development, 74. *See also* Human development
Distributive justice norms, 16–18
Dynamic patterns, 56
Dynamical systems: cohesiveness in, 58, 59; comparison and, 61; human development as, 55–58, 64, 67; implication of, 66–68; interdependence as, 62–63, 66; interdependence in, 58; overview, 60–61; reciprocity in, 56; self-organization and, 58–60; trust and, 56; uneasy coalitions in, 66, 67. *See also* Communal relationships; Exchange relationships

Empathy, 14
Equity norms, 8
Equity theory, 44–45

SINGLE ISSUE SALE

For a limited time save 10% on single issues! Save an additional 10% when you purchase three or more single issues. Each issue is normally $28⁰⁰.

Please see the next page for a complete listing of available back issues.

Mail or fax this completed form to: Jossey-Bass, A Wiley Company
989 Market Street • Fifth Floor • San Francisco, CA 94103-1741

CALL OR FAX

Phone 888-378-2537 or 415-433-1740 *or Fax* 800-605-2665 or 415-433-4611 *(attn customer service)*

BE SURE TO USE PROMOTION CODE DF2 TO GUARANTEE YOUR DISCOUNT!

Please send me the following issues at $25²⁰ each.

(Important: please include series initials and issue number, such as CD88)

1. CD _____

_____

_____

$ _____ TOTAL for single issues ($25²⁰ each)

_____ LESS 10% if ordering 3 or more issues

_____ SHIPPING CHARGES: SURFACE   Domestic   Canadian
                                    First Item $5.00 $6.50
                                    Each Add'l Item $3.00 $3.00
                For next-day and second-day delivery rates, call the number listed above.

$ _____ TOTAL (Add appropriate sales tax for your state. Canadian residents add GST)

❑ Payment enclosed (U.S. check or money order only)

❑ VISA, MC, AmEx, Discover Card # _____ Exp. date _____

Signature _____

Day phone _____

❑ Bill me (U.S. institutional orders only. Purchase order required)

Purchase order # _____
    Federal Tax ID. 135593032   GST 89102 8052

Name _____

Address _____

_____

Phone _____ E-mail _____

For more information about Jossey-Bass, visit our website at: www.josseybass.com

OFFER EXPIRES MAY 31, 2002.   **PRIORITY CODE = DF2**